DYING

With

Grace

J U D S
C O R N V

Charisma
HOUSE
A STRANG COMPANY

DYING WITH GRACE by Judson Cornwall
Published by Charisma House
A Strang Company
600 Rinehart Road
Lake Mary, Florida 32746
www.charismahouse.com

Unless otherwise noted, all Scripture quotations are from the King James Version of the Bible.

Scripture quotations marked NAS are from the New American Standard Bible. Copyright © 1960, 1962, 1963, 1968, 1971, 1972, 1973, 1975, 1977 by the Lockman Foundation. Used by permission. (www.Lockman.org)

Scripture quotations marked NIV are from the Holy Bible, New International Version. Copyright © 1973, 1978, 1984, International Bible Society. Used by permission.

Scripture quotations marked NKJV are from the New King James Version of the Bible. Copyright © 1979, 1980, 1982 by Thomas Nelson, Inc., publishers. Used by permission.

Scripture quotations marked TLB are from *The Living Bible*. Copyright © 1971. Used by permission of Tyndale House Publishers, Inc., Wheaton, IL 60189. All rights reserved.

Cover design by Karen Grindley

Library of Congress Cataloging-in-Publication Data
Cornwall, Judson.
  Dying with grace / Judson Cornwall.
    p. cm.
Includes bibliographical references.
  ISBN 1-59185-453-9 (pbk.)
  1. Death—Religious aspects—Christianity. I. Title.
BT825.C67 2004
248.8'6—dc22
                                          2003026542

04 05 06 07 08 — 987654321
Printed in the United States of America

Contents

Foreword

The Bible says that "it is appointed unto men once to die, but after this the judgment" (Hebrews 9:27). However, we as believers often have very little preparation for that eventuality, which none of us will avoid.

Our culture doesn't like to speak about death; in fact, we try to perpetuate youth as if we'll live forever. Even Christians seem to avoid the subject. When's the last time you heard a sermon on the subject other than at a funeral?

Now we have Judson Cornwall's book *Dying With Grace*. He writes about his own experience of being told by the doctors that he had only three months to live. You may have been told that recently, and you are searching for answers. Or perhaps you have a loved one who has just been told that he is to die, and you don't know what to do.

In either case you can learn from Judson's experience. For one thing, as I write this, his three-month death sentence has now turned into more than three years. So there is hope that your life might be extended. In his book, Judson grapples with the same emotions that you and your loved ones feel, and he has made the preparations that you will need to make for that inevitable day. But even more important than the feelings and preparations, he deals with the spiritual aspects of getting ready to meet our Maker.

I have known Judson for nearly twenty years. I have loved him as a spiritual father. After he had written the book, it was important for me to go to visit him at his home in Phoenix one last time, to pray for him and to also ask him to pray for me. It was a very meaningful, touching moment that I will never forget.

For those who are watching loved ones die, it is important to know how they feel, what they appreciate, and what they don't. Judson has been a teacher for decades, and now he teaches us how to die.

When my father died seven years ago, it was quick and unexpected. So while he was ready legally and financially to die, and ready also to meet God, none of us were able to grapple with the emotional aspects. Judson's book would have helped me at the time.

It would have also helped my family to deal with the death of my father-in-law nine years ago. His death came after a long seven-year period of debilitation from a stroke—one that did not kill him, but that kept him from living a normal life. During that period, even though we knew he didn't have long to live, and even though we were called to his bedside several times as if it were his last moments, some of the family never really knew how to grapple with the subject of his death.

I was deeply touched as I read this book and as I shared those precious moments with Judson. I hope that pastors and other professionals will use the book for counseling and for helping people to get ready for what we must all prepare for. I hope that you are similarly moved and helped by this book so that you know how to minister to others when they are dying, and so that some day you might also be able to, like Judson, die with grace—"surpassing grace God has given you. Thanks be to God for his indescribable gift!" (2 Corinthians 9:14–15, NIV).

—STEPHEN STRANG

Experiencing Grace to Live and Grace to Die

> I have fought a good fight, I have finished my
> course, I have kept the faith.
> —2 TIMOTHY 4:7

I'm dying! The doctor told me so, and, unless I was so sedated as to misunderstand him, I heard him tell my wife and daughter to take me home from the hospital and prepare for my imminent death. He assured them there was nothing they could do for me. My cancer had won the battle.

By the time you read this, I will probably be dead. But, of course, three years ago I was given only three months to live, and I'm still here, so, when you read this, maybe I will still be learning to die with grace.

Have you just learned that you are terminally ill? I know what that feels like. Do you have a loved one who has only a short time to live, and you don't know what to do? If so, I can show you the way. Are you a pastor who is grappling with how to minister to the ill or to comfort the grieving or even to prepare your congregation—no matter what age— for heaven? If so, I have been teaching and writing for seventy years—and I now have intimate, firsthand knowledge on the subject of dying, so let me show you the way.

If you don't know how to cope with death, it's no surprise. Our culture won't deal with death. One hundred years ago people were free to discuss death. Even the literature of that day dealt with the subject of death so often that it was often morbid. But those Victorians would not talk about sex. Today, nearly everyone talks about sex, but no one talks about death.

Death is inevitable. "And as it is appointed unto men once to die, but after this the judgment" (Hebrews 9:27). But even in the church, few teach on it.

When was the last time you heard a sermon on heaven? Or hell? Or death? But I know you have heard lots of sermons on grace...on believing in yourself...and on how God wants you to prosper. None of that will do you any good in the hereafter.

For the last seventy years I have been preaching—first as a boy preacher in the Great Depression and later as a pastor and traveling minister in the Charismatic community. I have taught on praise, prayer, God's Word, marriage, and many other topics. Now, on my deathbed, I want to leave a legacy so you and your loved ones can be guided step by step through the process and so you will understand what to expect on the other side.

I want to offer people a sense of value in passing into death. I want to help them to remove the fear so often attached to our thinking when it comes to death, and replace it with a response of joy. It should be a joyful occasion when a Christian dies—not a time for weeping and wailing.

People like Bill Bright, Derek Prince, Fuchsia Pickett— and, shortly, myself—receive a glorious promotion into the very presence of our Lord Jesus Christ. The funeral of a Christian is a day of victory, a time to gather around the casket and rejoice. I want the words people say as they stand before my casket to be, "Judson finally has made it into the presence of his Lord and Savior, Jesus Christ." I want them to rejoice, to celebrate my arrival into the eternal presence of God.

I want the people who read this book to recognize that they have an appointment with death—an appointment that cannot be canceled by anything they could do or say. But that appointment is not something they should fear; it is something that could fill their hearts with joy. That's my goal for writing this book—to make death a victorious experience.

The day I settled comfortably into my bed at home after arriving home from the hospital "to die," Paul's closing words as he came to the end of his appointed time on this earth came to my mind: "I have fought a good fight, I have finished my course, I have kept the faith" (2 Timothy 4:7). During my more than seventy years of ministry, I have used this Scripture passage for funeral discourses to honor servants of God whose course was finished. Now I visualize it being used at my own funeral. It was a comforting thought as I tried to accept the death sentence I had just received that day, and it comforts me still.

When my long-time assistant Terri Gargis was asked to say what she had observed about the dying process in me, she responded: "It's been different with Judson, because all the time he's been dying, he's been keeping the joy of the Lord. He is dying with grace, and he does it with joy." My prayer is that after reading this book, that same experience will be yours when God comes to escort you to your heavenly home.

DYING WITH GRACE

You see, I believe that just as He gives us a grace to live, God gives us a grace to die. Dying is a part of living. It is the finality. It gets us out of this life on earth so that we can enter our eternal life in heaven. Death is not a cessation of life—it is merely a stepping into the next realm, into the divine, heavenly realm, and God will give me—and you—grace to take each step from this life to eternal life.

KEY PRINCIPLE

Great reward is promised to those
who love His appearing.

There is laid up for me the crown of righteousness, which the Lord, the righteous Judge, will award to...all who have loved His appearing.

—2 TIMOTHY 4:8, NAS

CHAPTER 1

Exiting a Successful Life

As the hart panteth after the water brooks, so
panteth my soul after thee, O God. My soul
thirsteth for God, for the living God: when
shall I come and appear before God?

—PSALM 42:1–2

I have spent my life in fulfilling, God-given ministry. It
has been my desire to serve God on earth, just as it is
my desire to serve Him in heaven. I suppose it is very
natural to look back to remember and evaluate your life
when you receive a death sentence as I did, and I did what
was natural. Before exploring with me other principles I
have learned regarding the amazing grace God gives for
dying, I invite you to follow briefly my journey backwards,
reviewing with me the successes and satisfaction God has
given me in life.

One of the principles that can guide our lives as
Christians is the knowledge that God has promised
great reward to those who live their lives with a great
anticipation of the time when they will meet Him face
to face. At the beginning of this chapter you read the

1

verse: "There is laid up for me a crown of righteousness, which the Lord, the righteous Judge, will award to...all who have loved His appearing" (2 Timothy 4:8, NAS). I eagerly look forward to heaven—not merely because I will receive my Lord's reward, but because I long passionately to be in His presence, to meet Him face to face. As I take you along on my backwards journey through life, may you find ways to let your longing to see Jesus guide the steps you take on your own journey to a face-to-face eternal encounter with your Lord.

I am a preacher's kid who was saved at age three, filled with the Spirit at age six, and started preaching when I was just seven years old. Boy and girl ministers were quite a novelty during the depression years; people were fascinated with children who could preach the Word.

I remember, as a little boy, standing on a box behind pulpits in churches of different denominations sharing the little bit I knew about God and His Word. The people responded to the wonderful promises of God proclaimed through my childish expression; the results were good. The Bible works even when it is declared through the lips of a small child. Hallelujah!

LEAVING A LEGACY~*Thank you so much for the rich deposit that you left in my life. You are truly a "masterpiece."*

To appreciate more fully this part of my journey, we need to take a giant step forward across more than seventy years. In response to a telephone call from my brother Robert, who was my father's pastor at that time, I left a conference in New York State where I was ministering and traveled to my father's bedside in Salem, Oregon. I arrived to find that Dad was failing rapidly.

He was so weak that he could barely whisper, so communication was difficult and very one-sided. But his tears of joy upon seeing me communicated much more than words could have. After some preliminary conversation, my father pulled my head down so he could whisper in my ear.

"Judson," he said, "I need to explain something to you." I crawled onto his bed and tucked closely beside him.

"You must have wondered through the years why I never helped you get preaching invitations when you were a boy," he whispered.

"Yes, Dad," I replied, "I have often wondered why you never made a phone call on my behalf or would not at least drive me to churches that had invited me to speak. I concluded, in my boyish mind, that you must be ashamed of me."

"That's not even close to the truth," Dad responded. "In fact, your mother and I were very proud of you."

"Then why didn't you help me with my boyhood ministry?" I asked.

"Judson," Dad continued, "the Lord allowed me to see a mature ministry He was developing in you. It would have been to my financial advantage to travel with you and promote you as a boy preacher. But if I had secured your success as a boy preacher, people would not have accepted you as an adult minister; they would not allow you to grow up into your true ministry. Think about the boys and girls whose preaching was widely accepted in those days. Are any of them in the ministry today?"

Neither of us could think of one person who matured into adult ministry after beginning as a "famous" child preacher. Grateful for his explanation after all those years, I kissed my father and thanked him for his sensitivity to God's Spirit and for allowing me to develop quite normally into manhood without hindering the destiny that God had ordained for me.

As a young man, I was very active in my father's church, serving as the youth leader, song leader, and the occasional guest speaker. I was also the district youth director. My life was totally involved in the work of the church during my high school years—so much so that my high school graduation was an anticlimactic event for me. I was already enrolled in Southern California Bible College in Pasadena, California, and could hardly wait to move onto campus. I wanted to get on with my destiny and calling, which my godly parents had nurtured so carefully.

Setting My Life Course

Since I had been so heavily involved in my father's ministry and in Bible study during youth, many of the freshman college courses seemed somewhat anemic and elementary to me. Accommodating my situation, the administration graciously allowed me to take some sophomore classes during my first year. I was also chosen to be a speaker during choir tours, which gave me a wonderful opportunity for continuing to develop my teaching ministry. My studies and the ministry opportunities consumed a great deal of my time that year—but not all of it.

I still found time to pursue my courtship of Eleanor Louise Eaton, whom I married at the end of my freshman year. My successful courtship with Eleanor has proved to be the most valuable "course" I mastered during my years at Southern California Bible College.

After college, Eleanor and I accepted a call to pastor a small church in the lumber town of Stirling City, California. That little congregation of lumberjacks and mill hands may have taught me more than I taught them. It was a very small beginning, but it was a beginning. It marked the initiation of my ministry as a pastor, a ministry

I would continue for the next forty years.

God blessed me with fruitful years as a pastor to the four churches I served during those four decades, enabling me to teach the Word of God diligently along with the other responsibilities of pastoral ministry. And in addition to pastoral duties, I built new church buildings twice—supervising their construction and successfully using volunteer labor to accomplish this gargantuan task. The blessing of God on these years of ministry brought me great satisfaction in life.

WINDS OF CHANGE

My years of pastoral ministry were preparing me for later ministry of which I was not aware. The ever-increasing challenges it presented were each destined to increase my level of maturity, preparing me for the "mature ministry" my father had foreseen since I was a child.

When the Charismatic movement began to sweep this nation during the 1960s, my teaching ministry became very desirable to many churches and conference ministries. I began to receive so many invitations to minister to the body of Christ through various conferences and conventions that I no longer had the sufficient time required to adequately pastor my congregation in Eugene, Oregon. It seemed only fair to resign and let my church call another pastor to shepherd them. This was a big step of faith for me, requiring that I leave a "secure" ministerial and financial base, but God proved His faithfulness to fulfill His call on my life.

LEAVING A LEGACY~*Thank you for the rich insights and revelations that you have given. I have seen more of the Father's love through your services.*

I was commissioned by the Lord to trust Him alone to open doors for ministry. So for the next twenty years, I never wrote a letter or made a phone call asking for an opportunity to minister anywhere. And as God faithfully gave opportunities for ministry, I always received more invitations than I could accept.

EXPANDING AVENUES OF MINISTRY

When I began to travel in ministry, I considered myself a virtual "unknown." But before long, invitations to camp meeting and conference ministry continued to pour in as people who attended my conferences shared tapes of my services with people in other locations. As a result, I was invited to minister widely throughout Europe, South America, Asia, Australia, New Zealand, and several of the smaller island nations as well as receiving invitations to minister in almost every state of our nation.

Then, during the first years I traveled in ministry, several publishers pursued me, asking me to write a book for them. I protested that my traveling ministry schedule did not allow time for writing, but they assured me that I could squeeze a little time into it for this task. At their suggestion, I discovered that carrying a portable type-writer (and later, a laptop computer as technology advanced) with me gave me time to write while on air-planes, in airports, in hotels, and almost anywhere when I had time to sit and "wait."

For a while, every book I wrote was immediately snatched up by one of the newer Christian publishers. By the time my doctor declared that my death was imminent, I had written and published fifty books, and they were all doing quite well in the marketplace.

In many ways, my evolving experience in writing books has paralleled my growing relationship with Jesus Christ.

The first book I wrote, *Let Us Praise*, was written at a time when the church was just beginning to learn how to be comfortable with bold, unfettered expressions of adoration and praise offered to the Lord. As praise began to permeate my own life, I moved into a deeper, more intimate relationship with God, which helped me to write books like *Let Us Draw Near* and *Let Us Abide*. One book led to another, and soon I was producing three books a year. The Lord blessed them, and He is still blessing the lives of people through my books. And as I grew in my own relationship with God, He enabled me to express what I had learned through my teaching and through my books.

I am sure it came as a surprise to many, as it did to me, that yet another book is proceeding from my "pen," after receiving a sentence of imminent death from my physicians. It seems right, however, to continue to share with the body of Christ what I am learning on this perplexing journey through "the valley of the shadow of death," which is for all of us a culminating part of our journey through life.

GREATER RESPONSIBILITY
WITH GREATER MATURITY

I did not submit this section in my original manuscript. However, at the insistence of my editor, who has personally witnessed my last thirty years of ministry, I am delighted to acknowledge a God-given dimension of ministry and responsibility in the body of Christ for which I did not seek, and which has indeed been very satisfying to me.

It has been many years now since younger ministers began looking to me for more input than simply my role as a teacher in the body of Christ. They were seeking someone who had "been there" as a pastor who could mentor them and help them with difficult situations they were facing for which they had received no training. They were looking for a spiritual father.

Then the Lord began speaking through His prophets that the body of Christ needed "fathers and mothers in Israel" to whom a younger generation could look for mature guidance and wisdom. Many younger ministers began to declare to me that I was a spiritual father to them and to their ministry.

This facet of my calling has been a humbling and awesome recognition of God's favor, which has involved me in hours of counseling with brokenhearted ministers suffering the attacks of the enemy against their churches and in their personal lives. And it has given me great satisfaction to see God intervene many times, not only to comfort distressed ministries, but also to give solutions, redeem lives, and rescue churches from the clutches of the enemy.

There have been wonderful times of celebrating milestones of ministers' successful journeys as well of those who have become sons and daughters in the faith to me. To honor them, I am delighted to acknowledge that God has made me to be a "father in Israel" to those who asked for that relationship. The satisfaction I have received through these relationships can be matched only by the wonderful gifts God gave to my wife, Eleanor, and me in our own family.

LIFE SATISFACTION— MORE THAN MINISTRY

This chapter is supposed to establish that I have had a successful and satisfying life; yet so far I have confined my remarks to the satisfaction I have received from my God-given ministry. It is only fair to say that due to the graciousness and deep abiding love that my wife,

Eleanor, has had for me, I am still the husband of one wife. She has had grace to share with me in my ministry, while at the same time making our home the center for her God-given ministry.

As a result, our three daughters—Dorothy, Jeannie, and Justine—are all committed Christians and loving wives who have, in turn, raised their children to love the Lord. Two of our girls are in full-time Christian ministry, and our youngest daughter loves the Lord passionately, ministering to Him melodiously with an angelic voice. God graciously gave us the unspeakable satisfaction of sharing the successes and challenges of life with our own very special family.

It would require an entire book to share the blessings of this fulfilling and challenging life God gave to our family. In eternity, without constraints of time or space, we will be able to speak of these mercies of God. I can only say here that I am deeply grateful for the grace, love, and forgiveness with which He has blessed these dearest of relationships.

By nature I am a forward-looking person. I have not spent much time looking backward, but the finality of the statement "You have terminal cancer with less than a month to live" took all thoughts of future ministry out of my mind faster than a windstorm can distribute a pile of leaves. I didn't have a future in my life anymore. I could only reminisce.

It didn't take very long before I found myself burdened with the past. I tended to reflect more on my failures than on my successes. I saw hundreds of places where I could have done so much better. The enemy of my soul began to feed my memory circuits with my failures and with the times I settled for God's "good" rather than to persevere into His "best."

In His marvelous mercy the Lord began to redirect my thoughts from my lifetime exit to His eternal appearing. What He had in store for me was far more excellent than anything I could ever have done for Him. That longing to serve Him and, someday, ultimately to spend an eternity with Him surfaced again within my spirit. It was the longing that had guided my steps through life, provided balance in moments of earthly victory and earthly defeat, and would now soon usher me into His presence.

To that end I am filled with expectation because I have lived my life fully, though not perfectly, as one who loves "His appearing." What about you? Can you, with Paul and with me, say with assurance, "'Henceforth there is laid up for me a crown of righteousness' because I 'love His appearing'"?

KEY PRINCIPLE

God's presence brings His provision
into every season.

Yea, though I walk through the valley of the shadow of death, I will fear no evil: for thou art with me; thy rod and thy staff they comfort me.

—PSALM 23:4

CHAPTER 2

Entering a New Season

Thy way is in the sea, and thy path in the great
waters, and thy footsteps are not known.
—PSALM 77:19

It was just a routine physical examination, but that ordi-
nary visit to my physician opened the door for me to
enter a season of life I had never experienced before. It
was one where I would learn to depend completely upon
the presence and the provision of God. Before this season
I had a head knowledge of the spiritual principle upon
which I have based this chapter: God's presence brings
God's provision into every season. Once I stepped into this
new season in my life, I would develop a heart dependence
upon those words. It would be a season that brought great
change to my life, but it would also be a season when,
through prayer and utter dependence upon the provision
of God, great faith would be released in my life.

Since God is "the author and finisher of our faith"
(Hebrews 12:2), we need to spend time in His presence to

receive great faith for His provision. As I tell you of the events that caused me to step into this new season of life, I want you to recognize that it is through prayer that I have been brought into God's presence, which has enabled me to have the faith to believe Him for His provision.

When prayer brings us into the presence of God and our spirits get quiet enough to hear the voice of God speaking to us, we will discover all that He intends to do, and our faith is magnified beyond controllable proportions.[1] All the provisions of Christ's atonement flow to individuals through the energy of faith. The indwelling Holy Spirit and all forgiveness, cleansing, regeneration, and answers to prayer are received by faith. God has not provided an alternative way. This necessary faith is a gift of God, and it is a miracle. It is the ability God gives us to trust His Son.[2]

I would need to trust Christ in this new season of life, and you will need to trust Him when you enter seasons requiring His presence and provision to lift you above the circumstances facing you.

That routine physical examination had a not-so-routine revelation. It revealed that I had an unusually high PSA number. "Not to worry," the doctor said. "We can easily handle this with a series of radiation treatments."

So I canceled my ministry schedule for six weeks and faithfully gave myself to the radiation gun. It seemed to do the job, but when I returned for my six-month checkup, my PSA number was higher than before.

"This happens sometimes," the urologist said. "I recommend that we remove your testicles. Prostate cancer feeds on the testosterone that is produced in them. Remove the manufacturing plant, and you'll get rid of your cancer problem."

This solution sounded rather severe to me, so I took my problem to another doctor, who recommended the same procedure. Since this surgery would mark the end of my "manhood," I felt my wife should agree with my decision. When I talked it over with her, she responded that she preferred living with a limited husband to becoming a widow. So I surrendered myself to the surgeon's knife, and through prayer I surrendered myself to the presence and provision of my Lord.

After my surgery had been completed, the surgeon assured me, "That's the end of your cancer problem."

And I believed him.

Still the pain persisted. Months went by as I maintained my traveling and teaching schedule, but the pain made it more and more difficult to continue to function in my ministry lifestyle. Because standing was so painful to me as I ministered, congregations allowed me to preach from a sitting position.

LEAVING A LEGACY~*You've been on our hearts and minds, and our love and prayers are with you each and every day.*

Still, it was obvious to everyone that something was terribly wrong, even though the doctors had declared that the surgery would end the cancer problem. In spite of their optimistic prognosis, I had "inside" information—and it was not positive.

Much prayer from many beloved friends and family was offered to God for my healing. I was anointed and prayed for with loving hands laid on me as I stood, sat, knelt, and lay down. Concerned persons gave me the testimony of their miraculous healing or shared the healing a friend had received. I did everything I knew to do to enter into a healing touch from Jesus, but I continued to feel more miserable as my physical condition deteriorated.

It is at times like these when we must maintain our faith in the provisions of God for every season. How grateful I was in these moments for the blessed "Helper," the interceding Holy Spirit sent by Christ to walk with us through each season of our lives. Though I didn't know how to fully express my feelings about my deteriorating health to God, the Holy Spirit does. He can wondrously thank God for present provision while crying out for more and higher provisions, found only in the divine presence. The prayer we do not know how to pray is prayed through us by the Spirit.[3]

In my book *The Secret of Personal Prayer*, I included this paragraph:

> When Paul wrote, "Likewise the Spirit also helps in our weaknesses. For we do not know what we should pray for as we ought, but the Spirit Himself makes intercession for us with groanings which cannot be uttered" (Romans 8:26), he used the Greek work *sunantilambano*. We translate it "helps." It is really three words put together: *sun*, "together with"; *anti*, "over against"; and *lambano*, "to take." The combined word speaks of a person coming to another's aid by taking hold of the load he is carrying and helping to ease the burden; he does not take the entire load, but he helps carry it.[4]

Oh, how I needed the Holy Spirit to help me carry the burden of my health issues. I had no alternative but to trust His help to bring me into the provision of God for this season. I did not know the answer—but I trusted the source of my answer. You can do the same in your season of distress.

ANOTHER PROGNOSIS

When I flew home from a series of services in Fort Worth, Texas, my brother Jim, who is my pastor, met me at the airport and took me directly to the emergency room of our local hospital. He made a short stop at my home to explain to my wife what was happening. I hoped that all the doctors would find would be severe constipation, which they could treat by purging my system and then send me home.

Dreamer!

As it turned out, I was admitted to the hospital and submitted to a thorough medical examination for the next several days. Doctors and nurses took x-rays, did a CAT scan, and performed a whole battery of other medical tests. It seemed to me that if there was a hole in my body, they stuck something in it, and if there was no hole, they made one! I soon lost track of days and nights in this seemingly endless regimen of modern technology invading my life. I became a human pincushion for needles, and I became an expert pill popper. For the convenience of the medical staff, I was heavily medicated.

After nearly a week, I was suddenly released from the hospital. That was when the attending physician gave his ultimatum to my wife and my youngest daughter. He was not a person to mince words. In a matter-of-fact manner, he told my wife bluntly, "I'm sending your husband home to die. He is full of cancerous tumors, and there is nothing more we can do for him." He indicated that it would likely be no more than three weeks before I died.

My oldest daughter, who is a registered nurse, had already arranged for a local hospice service to care for me until I died. The papers were signed before I left the hospital, and the necessary equipment was waiting for me when I got home. Within days, I had a wheelchair, an oxygen machine, a walker, and other tools that made it easier for my wife to care for me. They also assigned a hospice nurse to me. Without her wonderful help in those first few days at home,

I may not have made it. I was weak; I was immobile; I was breathing with the help of oxygen; and all expectations were for my imminent death.

It would be hard to describe my feelings at that time. For one thing, it was my wife who received my death sentence for me—I was so out of it at that moment due to all the medication I had been given that I didn't hear it delivered from the doctor's mouth. But in those next few days when I did think about it, the feelings that I had were not fear; it was just: "This is it! I'm going to transport myself from this realm to the next realm."

Because my life has been focused on prayer and service to my Lord, I had an inner assurance that God would be with me and that He would provide for all my needs, just as He always has. It wasn't a "hands-off, accept whatever comes" kind of response on my part. Rather, it was a deep abiding faith in the Lord who had been my friend and companion through all of my life.

If God is your friend and companion, then you can trust Him with every circumstance of your life...even the most distressing, uncontrollable ones that threaten your very life...even when you receive a death sentence as I did. Turn to Him in prayer. The Holy Spirit who indwells your human spirit is able to interpret to God your spirit's most inarticulate longings. Prayer is no mere human activity. God Himself intercedes for us in heaven, and He prays through us on earth. Even when we do not know for what or how to pray, our human deficiency is supplemented by divine power as the Holy Spirit takes up the heavy end of our prayer burden and prays it through with us, "according to the will of God" (Romans 8:27).[5]

LEAVING A LEGACY ~ *We stand beside you with our love and prayers and ask our precious Lord to pour out on you all that you need in this hour.*

Beyond question, one of the important ministries of the Spirit is that of aiding us in prayer. Aiding—not replacing.

STRUGGLING WITH HEAVENLY VISIONS

As I returned home and began to deal with this death sentence, I thought that even God had confirmed this imminent reality to me, giving me a vision that was very real to me. As I lay in my bed, the vision began to unfold. I viewed myself in a very large room, somewhat like the waiting room at the hospital. I was seated with many other persons who were also waiting. From time to time, a door would open, and a person clothed in white and holding a clipboard would step into the room and read off a name. The man or woman whose name was called quickly walked over to the person in white and was then escorted out of the waiting room. I expected my name to be called next, but it was never called. When I came to myself, out of the vision that was so real to me, I was very disappointed but filled with hopeful expectation.

Shortly after that vision, I had another one in which I saw my godly mother-in-law, who has been in heaven for some years, peer around an open door with a most beckoning smile on her face. I accepted her appearance as a challenge, determined to go with her into heaven. Everything in me wanted to respond positively to that comforting invitation.

As I look back to those days more than two and a half years ago, I wonder if I was too quick to accept the doctor's sentence. Three weeks have come and gone—over and over again. In fact, I'm on my way to three years since that day. I am what they call a *man of God*, and I have been a preacher for years. I believe in God, trust Him implicitly with my life, and am embarrassed that I was so quick

19

to embrace what the doctor had to say. Now, more than two years later, I'm still alive. What can I say? I never expected to be embarrassed to be alive, but I am.

Believing the report of the doctors regarding my imminent death (we did not allow for the now apparent intervention of God), my family sent out the message of the "death warrant" to friends and associates. They, in turn, spread the word to people within their circles of influence. Throughout my years of ministry, I have been amazed at the speed with which the message of death is transmitted, even before the advantage of e-mail. I have often mused that if the message of the gospel could be communicated with the same speed with which we communicate death messages, we would blanket the world with the gospel in less than a week's time.

The news of my impending death traveled quickly through telephone calls, the Internet, and personal letters. It wasn't long before my family received a few "condolence" messages, in sympathy for my passing, from across the United States and from Europe, Asia, Africa, and South America.

If you have received terrible news about your health that may be a death sentence like mine, my advice today is to not be too quick to accept it. Check it out with God. Now, like me, there may be absolutely nothing you can do to change a thing, but I believe that I—and you—would have had a much greater peace in my heart had I said, "No, this sentence hasn't come from God; this is a doctor's death sentence."

I have no desire to speak negatively about doctors. They say the things they say to their patients based on the results of their tests and their knowledge of what those tests show them. But accepting their words can utterly destroy your faith. How much better it is to go to God's

Word to see what it says. Base your prayers on the promises of God. Be assured that your prayers are not wasted effort. God is on the throne, and He is listening to His children on the earth. Trust Him with your impossible situation, and pray:

> Seeing then that we have a great High Priest who has passed through the heavens, Jesus the Son of God, let us hold fast our confession. For we do not have a High Priest who cannot sympathize with our weaknesses, but was in all points tempted as we are, yet without sin. Let us therefore come boldly to the throne of grace, that we may obtain mercy and find grace to help in time of need.
> —HEBREWS 4:14–16, NKJV

Praying that portion of Scripture will reassure you that you are not merely granted the right to speak; you are guaranteed a listening audience at the throne of grace.

We must pray God's promises if we want to be reassured of God's presence, His purposes, His power, and His provision. It is hearing what God has said—not God's hearing what we have said—that revives our courage. The person who is strong in the Word will be strong in faith, and the person who couples that strength in the Word with his or her praying will be a courageous warrior in spiritual conflict.[6]

PRECIOUS MOMENTS

I was not gaining strength or showing any other signs of improvement, so we gathered my family and near-relatives around my sick bed and shared together what I thought were final words before departing. Those precious

21

moments were always tender times of praise and expressed submission to the will of God. God even used this time to bring some reconciliation between a grandson and his estranged wife.

To be perfectly honest, I was not aware enough of my surroundings to know all that was going on. The medication was helping me cope with the pain levels, the oxygen being fed to me through tubes in my nose helped my breathing, my wife and nurse were caring for my physical needs, and my secretary was caring for the office business. All of life was resolved for me; I had only to breathe in and breathe out.

I had entered a new season of life—indeed, I had entered a season of death. As you continue reading about my journey through this season, I want to be able to impart to you the spiritual principles that have enabled me to find the comfort and consolation of God, which has sustained me, strengthened me, surrounded me with the miraculous presence of God, and satisfied me with joy and peace and grace abounding. Let God begin to minister to you in your circumstances right now, as you see His faithfulness unfold through the pages of my life.

1. Judson Cornwall, *The Secret of Personal Prayer* (Lake Mary, FL: Creation House, 1988), 113.
2. Ibid., 114.
3. Ibid., 95.
4. Ibid., 96–97.
5. Ibid., 98.
6. Judson Cornwall, *Praying the Scriptures* (Lake Mary, FL: Charisma House, 1988), 109–110.

KEY PRINCIPLE

Godly comfort is available from those
who have been comforted by God.

Blessed be God, even the Father of our Lord Jesus Christ, the Father of mercies, and the God of all comfort; who comforteth us in all our tribulation, that we may be able to comfort them which are in any trouble, by the comfort wherewith we ourselves are comforted of God.

—2 CORINTHIANS 1:3–4

CHAPTER 3

Encouragement Needed

But encourage one another day after day, as
long as it is still called "Today,"...
—HEBREWS 3:13, NAS

There is one spiritual principle that should be the
focus of all our endeavors to relate to one another
in times of trouble and distress. It is this: because
of the comfort and encouragement you have received
from God in your own moment of deep need, you must be
ready to offer that same comfort and encouragement to
your brothers and sisters in Christ who are experiencing a
time of deep need. There are dear friends in Christ who
have reached out in encouragement to me in this season,
and it has made all the difference for me!

In this chapter I want to help you find ways to be an
encourager to your brothers and sisters in Christ. I will
share some of the ideas for reaching out that have meant
the most to me. I will try to help you know some of the
things you can do to reach out, as well as giving you some

advice on things not to do. Ask God for His wisdom in everything you do, remembering that the goal of reaching out is to give comfort and consolation that is most appropriate for that person in his or her moment of deep need.

REACHING OUT WITH GOD'S CONSOLATION

Expressions of love

One dear sister, Essie Jackson, has sent me a card of encouragement at least every month, and sometimes more often, since her son, Bishop Harry Jackson, who considers me his spiritual father, told her about my illness. As I have assured her, this ministry of encouragement will have eternal rewards. The body of Christ needs many more "Barnabases"—that is, sons of consolation. May we learn to *comfort* rather than *condemn* one another in our seasons of affliction and perplexity.

Initially, Essie Jackson was not alone in sending messages of comfort. As the news began to spread about my terminal prognosis, flowers began to arrive copiously. Sometimes two delivery vans arrived at the house at the same time. Before long, my bedroom looked like a nursery, with plants, flower bouquets, ferns, candles, and floral arrangements everywhere. The aroma was delightful, and the visual effect was most relaxing, but the most important role these flowers played was the message they communicated—"You are loved." "God bless you." "We're standing with you."

How I needed this encouragement in my weakened, drugged, and pain-wreaked physical state. It was difficult for me to read, and even the usually pleasant task of eating was more of an effort than it was worth, but it took no real energy to hear the "voice" of the flowers. How I thanked God that some persons had learned the vocabulary of the plants and flowers. God certainly knew what He was doing when He created the flowers even before He created Adam. (Adam probably needed their encouragement before Eve came on the scene.)

My mail carrier will gladly attest that not everyone sent flowers. Every mail delivery was loaded with cards of encouragement. I was glad I had installed a larger mailbox shortly before I became ill.

I don't know who creates these cards of sympathy and verses of comfort, but the writers must have been through trying times themselves to be inspired with such words of comfort and grace. No college education could produce such compassionate writing.

I now have a large box filled with these cards. I don't know what I will ever do with them, but they have brought me such joy and comfort that it seems almost sacrilegious to dispose of them.

If you know someone who is struggling with a terminal illness—or a devastating life circumstance of any kind—reach out to that person with the encouragement of a card. It takes so little effort to do this, and the encouragement it gives to that person can do so much to lift the spirit and give hope in that dark place.

My assistant, Terri Gargis, was kept busy answering the phone as friends called to ask about me and to send their best wishes and promises to pray for me. Many of them offered to fly into Phoenix and pray for me in person. Some were very insistent, but we felt that their visits would drain me of what little strength I had at that time.

I must admit that I was overwhelmed by the many expressions of such outpouring of love during the first few months of my illness. Friends were not alone in this love expression. My own family, from my wife to my great-grandchildren, lavished love on me as well. My brothers and sister took time from their busy schedules to come to my bedside and pray for me. Grandchildren from the East Coast flew to my bedside, and my three daughters, who live here in Phoenix, were constantly sensitive to my needs.

My middle daughter, who is a seamstress, made me new nightgowns. My baby daughter saw to it that I had a lightweight Bible to read, and my oldest girl, the nurse, kept an eagle eye on my medication and care. All the while, my wife nearly exhausted herself caring for my physical needs of food, clothing, and shelter. I was floating in a sea of love. As I mentioned earlier, all that was expected of me was to continue to breathe in and breathe out.

There are so many ways that you can reach out to give God's love and hope to another. Be sure that you are aware of that person's physical limitations if you plan to make a personal visit or even a phone call. There are days when I simply do not have enough strength to receive a visit, and times when it simply is not practical or possible for me to talk on the phone. Check with the person's primary caregiver before you call or visit.

A new source of encouragement

When, in spite of doctors' expectations, I gained strength instead of expiring, I had to begin to reassess my role in life. Death was expected to come during the months of June or July, but those months passed, and the Christmas season was now looming on the horizon. By this time, I was strong enough to spend a few hours daily out of bed by using long extension tubes that carried oxygen from the machine to my nose. Though it was awkward, it let me out of my bedroom for short, refreshing periods of time.

Tea at the poolside was like a vacation at Niagara Falls, only closer and far less expensive. I could sit for a few hours in my comfortable lounge chair, from which I wrote this book, and interact with my family in surroundings far less threatening than the sick bed. My family and friends rejoiced that God seemed to be healing me—in His way and in His time.

You may find by checking with the caregivers for your sick friends that these moments away from the sick bed are ideal times for you to spend a small amount of time with your friend. These little oases of normalcy can help your friend to feel a part of everyone else's lives, and as though his or her illness, though a dominating circumstance, is not the only important facet of life. But be very aware of your friend's physical limitations, and do not allow your interaction to fatigue or cause physical discomfort.

Help for the caregiver

One of the greatest things that you can do to bring comfort to a family dealing with a major illness is to offer to help with the care of the sick person so that the primary caregiver can have some personal time. During the course of my illness, two of my grandsons have taken turns sitting with me on Sunday morning, thus freeing my wife to go to church. They usually slipped out to a restaurant to bring back a take-out lunch. These times have proven to be the best and most intimate fellowship I have had with these young men. I had watched them mature from boyhood into manhood, but I had not yet enjoyed fellowship with them as young men tackling the responsibilities of maturity.

LEAVING A LEGACY~*My words are seldom sufficient, but God's grace is always sufficient. I pray His love, peace, strength, healing, and grace over you and Mrs. Cornwall.*

The reverse of our deepened fellowship proved to be true as well. They expressed a personal joy at getting to have time with me on a "nonprofessional" level. They

29

seemed amazed that I had any knowledge of or interest in things outside the Bible, and they were pleased to discover that I subscribed to secular magazines. I'm afraid that I had come across to them as a "holy Joe" without meaning to.

There are many ways that you can provide comfort in this way. If it is not possible for you to actually provide relief by caring for the sick person for a short period of time, you can offer to run errands or help with housework or take in a home-cooked meal. The possibilities are endless for the creative ways that you can help provide much needed rest and comfort to a caregiver.

Expressions of thanks

The doorbell rang, and our living doorbell amplifier, Deacon, our dog, set up a barking barrage that we couldn't possibly overlook.

Eleanor went to the door as rapidly as possible and found the Federal Express employee standing there with a package. The two of us are still childlike enough to get excited when an unexpected box is delivered to us.

We tore the box open and pulled out a beautiful crystal eagle, mounted on a stand that could be lighted. There was an accompanying letter with the gift explaining that the International Third World Leaders Association, with headquarters in the Bahamas, had selected me to be one of their honorees at their 2002 convention.

I have served on the advisory committee with Dr. Myles Munroe for many years, but with my debilitating sickness, I had not been actively involved with this ministry for several of those years. Their gift and special invitation were a source of real joy, helping me to realize that I had not been forgotten.

It made me remember another event, which happened just days just before I entered the hospital. I had ministered last in Fort Worth, Texas. At the same time, a great worship conference was convening in that city. LaMar Boschman, on whose board I have also served for many years, had written to me earlier and asked if I could stop by the worship conference one evening. They wanted to present me with an award in honor of my being a pioneer in the praise and worship renewal here in America.

I responded positively. It was a humbling experience for me to receive a crystal award that evening as well, with a loving inscription on it. I find it interesting that God allowed me to receive this special honor just days before I received my death sentence and then allowed me to be honored again after I had lived twenty months beyond the "set time," with that sentence still unfulfilled.

Do I have to have these honors to continue on faithfully? I should hope not. I shared earlier how I had to learn anew the power of encouraging myself in the Lord, precisely through the power of praise. However, when the pain just will not subside, and the enemy of my soul whispers condemnation to me, declaring as well that my ministry is over, a special word of thanks like the one that came this morning by e-mail helps to infuse me with fresh courage. Today, a pastor with whom I have ministered on repeated occasions wrote:

> The flock still seems to be healthy, and we still walk in the influence that you so graciously deposited in our lives. You may not be able to visit us as in previous years, but [your] life and example continue....[You] are always a father and example to me.

For a brief moment after I read this pastor's expression of thanks, I did not walk stooped over from pain—I stood six feet tall. What comfort it was to know that ministry freely given is continuing to have an effect in the lives of God's children. Largely for this purpose I have given my life to the rigors of ministry.

In that moment I could identify with Paul (though I do not put myself in his league) when he wrote, "Now I praise you, brethren, that ye *remember* me in all things, and keep the ordinances, as I delivered them to you" (1 Corinthians 11:2, emphasis added). Paul lived in the same human flesh I do, and I am greatly encouraged to know that though my body may be largely incarcerated in this family room, what God has done through me in past seasons of ministry is still bearing fruit affectionately *remembered.*

Effectively handling expressions of thanks

It is obvious that God knows our inner needs even better than we do. It is seldom that an entire week goes by that we don't receive some form of communication, sharing what a blessing or challenge my books have been to individuals. It is comforting to know that though I may die, my ministry will live on, bearing fruit for eternity.

At the last major convention where I ministered before receiving my death sentence, the director of the conference had sheets of paper distributed to the attendees, and he requested that they write their testimony of how my ministry may have blessed them. These messages were put into a fancy box and given to me as a memorial. I must admit that I have not yet read all of them, but I have kept them in a safe place for my encouragement.

How thankful I am to God that my book on pride (actually, the theme is humility) had been released before these words of praise were bestowed on me.[1] I have reread that book recently, and the earnest prayer of my heart is that I will consistently place all these expressions of honor at the foot of Christ's cross. All we are and all we can do for eternity are only possible by the grace of God. It is imperative that we remember that.

Years ago, God taught me to consider all praise extended to me as gifts of flowers. I am to make a bouquet of the flowers, and I am allowed to smell them and enjoy them. But I must present the bouquet to Jesus before going to sleep in the evening. Personal praise received is a dangerous pillow on which to try to sleep. We will painfully discover the thorns on the stems of those "personal praise" flowers if we dare to hold them close.

How merciful God is to allow me to be reminded of past ministry and its positive effect on lives. Yet, even that kindness does not remove the pain of having no ministry in the present. Still, even in this the Spirit gently corrects me, reminding me that I am not *without* ministry—I simply have no *public* ministry. I have been challenged to be available to minister to everyone who comes to my house or who contacts me by phone or e-mail. It is interesting the ways this new phase of ministry has transpired.

I have also received many expressions of thanks in the personal notes that have been written on the cards that have been sent to me. I still get cards from people saying, "We love you." "We remember you." "Oh, how wonderful when you used to be able to come to our church." Those are so meaningful to me. For a person such as myself, a tremendously busy person used to traveling constantly, who was embraced by many and invited to many more places than I could ever travel to, these expressions are so fulfilling. When I am tempted to focus on the fact that I can no longer go anywhere, it means so much to get a note from a pastor, saying, "I just remember the last time you were with me. You taught on this or that, and what a blessing it has been to me." Even the notes that simply say,

"God bless you; we're remembering you," bring a fresh breath of hope to me.

I have chosen to share a few of these encouraging notes in this book, interspersing them throughout the chapters in a special format. These are not to remind myself—or you—of my own importance to others, but to demonstrate for you the kinds of simple, loving, faith-filled expressions of thanks you can give to a loved one during a time of illness or distress. Whom do you know today who could be greatly encouraged by receiving a similar note from you?

It is very important for people to contact their friends and loved ones who are sick and let them know they are loved. What a source of strength and encouragement that is.

Encouraging through God's Word

There are many people who encourage me by sending notes with Scripture verses for encouragement. There is nothing better than the Word of God to lift the human spirit and strengthen the soul, and it is important to note how much encouragement has come to me from the verses sent to me by others.

There are so many powerfully uplifting portions of Scripture that can be used to lift the spirits of a sick friend. When God gives you fresh revelation from His Word, pass that revelation and encouragement on to someone who desperately needs it. The psalmist David was greatly encouraged in times of great need by reading God's Word, and his psalms have, in turn, provided millions of people with encouragement—including myself. During this season of my life, I have often cried out with the psalmist: "Bless the LORD, O my soul, and forget not all his bene-

LEAVING A LEGACY~*We pray for God's peace and comfort to pour over you, surround you, and envelop you during this time.*

fits: Who forgiveth all thine iniquities; who healeth all thy diseases" (Psalm 103:2–3).

Encourage your friend with God's Word. How uplifting it would be to receive a card today with these words:

> Though the fig tree may not blossom, nor fruit be on the vines; though the labor of the olive may fail, and the fields yield no food; though the flock may be cut off from the fold, and there be no herd in the stalls—yet I will rejoice in the LORD, I will joy in the God of my salvation. The LORD God is my strength; He will make my feet like deer's feet, and He will make me walk on my high hills.
>
> —HABAKKUK 3:17–19, NKJV

WHAT NOT TO DO

For more than two years I suffered with cancer prior to receiving my death sentence. I openly shared my physical condition with congregations where I ministered. I sought to enlist their prayers. In retrospect, I believe that may not have been wise. But at the time, I felt I was taking the humble road by asking for help.

As a result of my openness about my disease, many sincere brothers and sisters certainly reached out to me with their attempts to help. Some prayed most earnestly for me in sympathetically identifying with my need for a healing touch from Jesus. Others almost stood in line to recommend various pills, vitamins, and mechanical devices I could wear, offering them as gifts or for sale. I received addresses as well of doctors in Canada and in Mexico who had clinics where all forms of cancer were being cured.

At first I resented these offers of "remedies," but the Lord let me get a glimpse of the love behind these friends' endeavors to help. So I learned to accept whatever they presented to me with as much sincere thanksgiving as I could muster. I took a few of these offered remedies to my family doctor, who said that perhaps they would work if I had enough faith in them. I told him that I preferred to rest my faith in the Word of God. He agreed with me that this was a wiser choice. I would include the sending of "remedies" and "cures" to a sick person in a category of things *not to do* if you are trying to encourage a sick person. Suggesting to a sick person that "if you want to get well, you should do such and such or take this or that medication" can be distressing, counterproductive to what his or her doctors are doing to treat the condition, and even guilt producing for the patient. The sick person is desperate for answers but must carefully and prayerfully entrust his or her care to a specialized care provider so focused treatment can be given. These volunteered remedies so often carry the unspoken assertion, "Well, if you *really* want to get well, you should be trying *this*." That can be very hurtful. I have felt this hurt, and I would counsel you to be sure you are not inflicting such hurt on your sick friends.

There is another kind of hurt that is often inflicted by well-meaning Christian friends. This is the projection of guilt upon a sick person. This can come as simply as merely saying to a sick friend, "Well, this is what I believe. If you will believe that too, then you will have the healing you want." Or it may come in the form of the more painful attack of accusing a sick person of having sin in his or her life that is responsible for the illness. I have had the following verse quoted to me more times than I want to think about: "So the curse causeless shall not come" (Proverbs 26:2). "Now search your heart, Brother Cornwall. There's hidden sin there somewhere," one person wrote to me. "God would never let this happen if there wasn't a reason for it."

That projection of guilt is totally unfair to a sick person. I have searched my heart in every possible way, and I can find nothing there that God is condemning me for. Please be certain that you never do this sort of thing with your sick friends. Even if you have every reason to believe there probably is guilt, be the Christian, and speak forgiveness to that person—not guilt!

When you have a loved one who is walking through the season of death, be aware that person is already dealing with emotions of confusion, discouragement, and doubt. Dealing with death raises so many questions for the person dealing with it—and for that person's loved ones.

In the next chapter we will look at some of the questions I have had—some with answers, and some that can only be answered by God when we see Him face-to-face. Hopefully, the things that I have learned about these issues will help you and your loved ones also.

---

1. Judson Cornwall, *Forbidden Glory: Portraits of Pride* (Hagerstown, MD: McDougal Publishing, 2001).

KEY PRINCIPLE

The tyrannical question "Why?" cannot always be answered; it must simply submit to worship.

Why art thou cast down, O my soul? and why art thou disquieted within me? hope thou in God: for I shall yet praise him, who is the health of my countenance, and my God.

—PSALM 42:11

CHAPTER 4

Endeavoring to Understand

> I will say unto God my rock, Why hast thou
> forgotten me? why go I mourning because of
> the oppression of the enemy?
>
> —PSALM 42:9

For many years I have enjoyed singing C. A.
Tindley's old gospel song "We'll Understand It
Better By and By." I have even gotten quite emotional anticipating this impending revelation of understanding that is to come. But my cancer is not in my "by
and by"; it is in my nasty here and now. And I don't
understand it one bit!

In this chapter I want to focus on a spiritual principle
that will help you in those times when you cannot understand what is happening to you one bit, either! This is it:
there will be times when you cannot find an answer for
the tyrannical question "Why?" In those times, do not
distress because you have no answers. Instead, simply
submit your situation—and your unanswered questions—
to worship. We will take a look at some of the questions

I have had during this season of my life. They are questions that you will have at times, as well. Recognize the value of submitting your questions to worship. I will help you find the way to do that—just as I had to do, and still must do, as I await the final release from my death sentence here on earth.

UNANSWERED QUESTIONS

"Why hasn't God healed me?"

"Why?" is one of the first questions we find coming from our lips when negative circumstances slam into our daily lives. As a Christian leader, I believe beyond any shadow of doubt that God heals—He healed in Old Testament times. He built His church on the cornerstone of healing. And He heals today.

To the children of Israel who had just been delivered from the stranglehold of slavery in Egypt, He counseled, "If thou wilt diligently hearken to the voice of the LORD thy God...I will put none of these diseases upon thee, which I have brought upon the Egyptians: for I am the LORD that healeth thee" (Exodus 15:26).

By His death on Calvary, Jesus Christ provided salvation and healing for His people. "Who his own self bare our sins in his own body on the tree, that we, being dead to sins, should live unto righteousness: by whose stripes ye were healed" (1 Peter 2:24).

Yet I am trapped in a terminal illness from which I could find no healing. I live inside this body, which feels as if it is betraying me. While I do not claim perfection, I do feel that with the help of the Holy Spirit, I have lived an exemplary life in public and in private. I have demonstrated the same faith and behavior in my home as I did in an auditorium filled with people. Yet, God has not healed me. If we believe that Christian behavior merits God's healing favor, I should be well. Why hasn't God healed me?

It doesn't help to have visitors voice their feelings of confusion over my sickness. I don't think there is any way that they can match my own confusion. None of this makes sense to me. I really don't know why God has not healed me. I join Job at this juncture of his experience.

There is something about suffering that most of us Christians don't understand. We see the dealings of God as being very temporal and that it is His blessed will to heal everyone. Yet the Bible speaks of fulfilling the sufferings of Christ. I am not sure we understand that very well. We feel there should be no suffering or pain, yet all through the Scriptures we see chosen ones of God enduring suffering and pain.

I have to leave this in the hands of God—and you will need to do the same when you cannot find answers to this question. Submit your questions to God, and follow the advice that Paul gave to young Timothy when he exhorted him to "fight the good fight of faith" (1 Timothy 6:12).

Even though faith is a divine energy that comes as a gift from God and is released in our believing, it has an enemy. Whether that enemy surfaces from within our lives or opposes us from without, the name of that enemy is *doubt*. Doubt is not unbelief; it is more a poor handling of belief. Doubt is uncertainty about God's promises; doubt lacks confidence in the God of those promises and considers their fulfillment very unlikely. Doubt puts our experience over against God's Word and trusts our reasoning more than the reality of God's Word. Doubt is always costly, but it is especially costly when it becomes a dominant force in the moment of crisis.[1]

The way to overcome the word of doubt is with the "word of faith" which "is near you, in your mouth and in your heart" (Romans 10:8, NKJV). Since faith flows when God speaks, we will do well to remain in His presence to hear His voice during the dark seasons when doubt demands an audience. If faith and doubt are mortal enemies, we need to have a constant increasing and strengthening of our faith, lest the doubts induced by our natural life overcome our faith in God. The more time we spend in God's presence, the stronger our confidence and trust in Him will become.[2]

"Why was my brother Robert healed and not me?"

Another question believers have in illness is this: "Why was so-and-so healed, but not me?" For example, the same month that I discovered that my PSA was high, I urged my brother Robert to have his PSA level checked. Not too surprisingly, his level proved to be higher than mine. His urologist recommended a different treatment than was given to me, and he was cured. Why him and not me? I don't see him as more godly than myself. I have no reason to believe that he is more faithful in tithing and giving than I am, or that his level of personal holiness is better than mine. Still, it seems that God has seen fit to spare him and leave me afflicted.

This is another question that arises in a moment of crisis, but we don't have an answer for it. God is sovereign, and He does as He wills to do. That isn't very satisfactory to twenty-first-century Christians. If healing is something the children deserve, then God doesn't have the right to heal one person and not heal another. If healing is receiving grace from God and is left to His will to give to whom He chooses, and to not give to another, then that becomes another issue. We Christians would do well to let God be God and stop trying to play His role.

We should seek Him earnestly for the best that He has, and then dare to trust Him to know what is the best. Is it just possible that sickness is the best for some people? We don't know what the spiritual needs of that person actually are. If, through sickness, God can form in me a Christian grace that He could not do with my good health, then God has a right to use any tools at His disposal to effect the grace He is wanting to perfect in me.

In God's view, insisting upon our own way is participating in the works of the devil. Since this is true, submission to the will of God becomes the first rule of Christian behavior. It will not always be easy, but it will always be right.[3]

There comes a time in our prayer lives when we cease dealing with our wills, wants, and wishes, and we face the will of God. When He impresses that will upon our hearts, we remain in His presence, allowing Him to communicate with us by His indwelling Spirit. We soften. Our wills crumble, and we, like Jesus, find ourselves saying, "Not my will, but Thine be done."[4]

LEAVING A LEGACY~*May God show you a glimpse each day of the glorious things He has in store for you.*

"How do I get rid of my anger and bitterness about being sick?"

During this painful season of trying to find reasons for my diagnosis of incurable cancer, I struggled with inner anger and bitter thoughts. Others were being healed. Persons for whom I prayed over the phone got healed, while I remained ill. I think it would have helped if God had given me a reason, but He remained silent. Graciously, He warmed my heart with His presence, but I wasn't hearing His voice during my Bible reading or in my prayer time. Perhaps I was too preoccupied with my pain and misery to hear the "still small voice" of the Master.

If you are struggling with trying to overcome anger and bitterness about your sickness, I think, first of all, you need to find out why you are angry. Do you feel that you deserve something better? If so, your resentment will eventually turn to anger and bitterness of spirit. The truth is, none of us get what we deserve. If we did, we would all be bound in hell.

If you will focus on God's blessings in your life instead of your sickness, then there will be rejoicing in that you are still alive instead of being angry and bitter. It's sad to spend our lives majoring on the negatives. God has done so much for us that we should be grateful and filled with thanksgiving for what He has done, rather than be resentful and bitter about what He has not done.

The antidote to anger and bitterness is thanksgiving. Perhaps one of the most positive by-products of giving thanks to God is that it refocuses our perspectives by causing us to look to Jesus. As we give thanks, we look away from self, from success, from failure, from ambition, and from circumstances. Thanksgiving moves us from negative thinking into positive thinking. Expressing thanks to God for what He has already done for you will release negatives from your heart and mind and replace them with positives.

In the passage where Paul exhorts us to pray with thanksgiving, he added, "Finally, brethren, whatever things are true, whatever things are noble, whatever things are just, whatever things are pure, whatever things are lovely, whatever things are of good report, if there is any virtue and if there is anything praiseworthy—meditate on these things" (Philippians 4:8, NKJV). When you are struggling with overwhelming feelings of anger or bitterness—put God to the test, and follow Paul's exhortation to pray in this manner. You will be glad that you did.

"Why doesn't God heal me through the anointing of someone like Benny Hinn?"

When some Christians find themselves ill with a threatening disease, they run from one healing evangelist to another looking for a healing. After all, doesn't God's Word promise believers that "they shall lay hands on the sick, and they shall recover" (Mark 16:18)? In another verse we read, "Is any sick among you? let him call for the elders of the church; and let them pray over him, anointing him with oil in the name of the Lord" (James 5:14).

Fortunately, we get two Christian channels on our cable television, and both channels carry the Benny Hinn program daily. I have known this dear brother from a distance almost from the beginning of his outstanding healing ministry. When he pastored a local church in Florida, I preached for him. And on a tour of Israel some years ago, we were both speakers at a conference in Jerusalem. I can attest that he is a gracious Christian gentleman with an obviously powerful anointing on his life and in his ministry.

During these months in which I have been gravely ill, I have listened to and watched his telecasts several times a day. I have wept as I have seen others dramatically healed. I have desperately sought to enter into the anointing I could see flowing to the vast gathering of persons in the large auditoriums he rents and to receive the anointing applied to the sick persons on the stage. When he prays for persons watching the telecast, I sit with my arms stretched toward the television and weep with anticipation as I enter into his prayer for the sick. I often sense God's presence, but not His healing power. I am filled with cancerous tumors at the beginning of the telecast, and they seem to be undisturbed at the end of it. God has not, so far, done for me what He has done for others.

I have known some of these men who are greatly used in divine ministries, and they are the first to admit that they don't understand why God heals one and not another. God is sovereign, and He will do as He chooses to do. If He chooses to work through the ministry of an anointed brother or sister, then hallelujah! If He chooses to *not* do it, He is still worthy of our praise and thanksgiving.

"How do I keep my circumstances from affecting my emotions?"

It is sad, almost pathetic, how we let circumstances color our application of Scripture to our lives. My "sense" of faith is merely a feeling—a sensation. Real faith is not involved with our emotions; it is totally involved with believing God and His Word. That involvement will affect our emotions, but the equation will not work in reverse. That is to say, faith in God and His Word can produce great inner feelings and emotional responses, but these feelings are not faith producers. I have proven that!

I know intellectually and experientially that emotional feelings will not produce faith. I explained this concept in my book on faith.[5] I have preached this truth throughout the world, teaching the reality that faith comes by hearing the Word of God (Romans 10:17). Faith and emotional feelings are two entirely different realities. But when the "problem" became mine and very personal, I sidestepped the truth of faith and responded to my illness in my emotions, instead of leaning in faith on the whole counsel of God.

I need to remind myself that I control my emotions; they do not control me. You will need to do the same. If I choose to give in to my negative circumstances, then I will probably be filled with anger, bitterness, and resentment. If I choose to control my emotions and focus on the goodness of God and on the positives, then I will be a rejoicing saint and not one who complains. We Christians focus so much on the negatives that we forget there are positives. Happy is the person who has learned to major in the positives in his life. Negative circumstances will produce negative emotions only if you allow them to do so.

When Jesus stood at the gravesite of His friend Lazarus, He said, "Father, I thank You that You have heard Me." Then He said, "Lazarus, come forth!" (John 11:41, 43, NKJV). The greatest miracles of the ministry of Jesus were performed after He gave thanks to the Father.[6]

Admittedly, however, present problems can so cloud our memories that we cannot recall any good thing that God has done for us. This is when we need to look at others and rejoice vicariously in what God has done for them. In times of pressure, when my spirit was so overwhelmed that I couldn't seem to find the presence of God during prayer, I have opened my Bible to the Book of Psalms and have paced the floor reading aloud while identifying with the psalm by saying, "Amen!" Invariably, I found myself praising the Lord and enjoying His presence in a very short time. This is one of the reasons that the Bible records so much of what God has done for and in persons. We can benefit from their relationships with Him.

Practice taking control of your emotions and being positive no matter what your circumstances.

"What sin of mine brought on the curse of sickness?"

Shortly after I was sent home to die, I received a brief card from a minister friend with whom I had ministered in a large convention just a month earlier. In an almost sticky-sweet manner, he challenged me to search my heart to find out why God had sent this affliction upon me. He reminded me that Scripture teaches, "Like a sparrow in its flitting, like a swallow in its flying, so a curse without cause does not alight" (Proverbs 26:2, NAS).

In my weakened physical condition, and with my body trying to cope with the morphine I was taking to modify my pain, I accepted this indictment. Responding emotionally, I felt this was the answer I sought—"The curse causeless will not come." My weary mind did not allow me to reach for any balancing Scripture verses. I immediately began a soul search with vigor for the cause of the curse. Where had I sinned so seriously that God had to afflict me with prostate cancer to bring me to repentance?

I can assure you that although you may be too weak to remember the names of your children, in your extreme weakness, you can easily remember past sins. The devil will see to that. His computer is always "on," and your file can be activated in a millisecond—or so it seems to me.

I was reminded of how critical I had been in public ministry about television preachers. Ironically, now I was listening intently to them to receive some spiritual food since I was unable to go to church for several months. You better believe that I asked God to forgive me for my expressed attitude toward them.

But healing did not come as a result.

I dug deeper into my memory circuits to uncover sins of action, attitude, or desire. Still the Holy Spirit did not respond to me. I was on my own as I dug into my past. The Spirit played ignorant about any of these things I was digging up.

One day in my prayer time, I probed way back into my past and uncovered a confessed sin of considerable magnitude. It was a sin that involved a person in a church I had pastored many years ago. I deeply hurt this person, and it was some time before healing could come to him. I had earnestly asked this person's forgiveness and asked forgiveness of all others who had been affected by my sin. God granted great forgiveness, and I walked in greater victory in Christ Jesus as a result.

In my desperate soul searching for a cause of my affliction, I rehearsed this sin episode in my memory circuits. What a mistake this was. The Holy Spirit rebuked me: "Judson, if you continue to uncover what the blood has covered, the righteous demands of the Law will yet reach out and condemn you. Never seek to uncover what Christ's blood has covered."

I had been through this kind of unhealthy introspection for years before and had used my experience as a sermon illustration on many occasions. But Satan does not give up easily. He loves to drag us through the muck and slime of sin, no matter how old it is or even when it has been forever forgiven by God.

God reminded me that He does not want to hear me talk about what He has put under the blood of Jesus. He has not only forgiven us, but according to the Scriptures, He has also forgotten our sins: "I, even I, am he that blotteth out thy transgressions for mine own sake, and will not remember thy sins" (Isaiah 43:25).

The Word of God declares, "As far as the east is from the west, so far hath he removed our transgressions from us" (Psalm 103:12). That's too far to be retrieved, even for cyberspace. When we "reconfess" sin from which Christ has already cleansed us, we put the sin on the table of God's remembrance to be dealt with again. How stupid!

That note was not the only one I received challenging me to search my heart for hidden sin. When I received others, I learned to make up my own melody based on David's Psalm 103:12 that reminds me that "as far as the east is from the west" are those sins lost in the sea of forgetfulness.

Those last few words became my source of victory. Confessed and forgiven sin should not be brought back to my conscious mind. Since I am now forgiven, I can praise God for forgiveness. Christ's vicarious work at the cross gives a reason for that praise.

"How do I avoid depression?"

As weeks stretched into months, which took me through the Christmas season, the number of cards from friends diminished, and plants stopped arriving, with only a few exceptions. I received less and less phone calls of encouragement, and even the e-mail contacts dwindled to but a few per day. This change was to be expected, but it induced a loneliness in me. I didn't realize how much I had come to lean on the encouragement that came from others in these ways.

When these expressions of love dwindled, I found myself in "withdrawal," not too unlike what a drug addict must feel when denied his drug of choice. Kind words of encouragement from others had strengthened me for months. Now I had a choice before me: *to slip into depression or learn to encourage myself*. I have wrestled with bouts of depression in my life, enough to know that I didn't dare give myself over to it again. Fighting these cancerous tumors and the pain they induce was enough. I didn't need to fight depression, too.

There was only one answer—I had to "relearn" to encourage myself. Now I could not settle for merely *reading* the Psalms; I needed to *live* them. I had to rediscover the power of praise. And I well knew that thanksgiving births praise, as David wrote:

> Thou hast turned for me my mourning into dancing: thou hast put off my sackcloth, and

girded me with gladness; to the end that my
glory may sing praise to thee, and not be
silent. O LORD my God, I will give thanks
unto thee for ever.

—PSALM 30:11–12

It was time for me to remember God's great goodness
to me the past few months. I was *alive*—in spite of the
doctor's predictions. I was strong enough to be out of bed
several hours at a time. The cards, letters, flowers, and
phone calls from individuals who said they were praying
for me blessed me.

As I reflect on this time, I found many reasons for
praising God. Like David I could cry, "The LORD hath
done great things for us; whereof *we are glad* "(Psalm
126:3, emphasis added). "Be glad, not sad" was God's
challenge to me. I understood the Scriptures were
instructing me to rule my emotions and not let them rule
me. I realized I had not yet faced a circumstance in life so
severe that I could not be glad in the Lord.

This was not the time for self-pity; it was the time to
praise God. So I did. I praised with my mouth, with my
mind, with my voice, and with melody. I praised with
body language, with the English language, and with the
language of the Spirit. I praised in the silence of the night
and in the noise of daily activities. And the more I praised,
the more encouraged I became.

To be perfectly honest, this praise did not always come
easily. Much of it was expressed through clenched teeth
and an inner feeling of hypocrisy, but it was expressed
nonetheless. God deserved the praise, and I desperately
needed to express praise. I knew it was my lifeline for living above depression at this juncture of my dying experience. In spite of the toll the disease had taken, I still had a

lot of life left in me, and that life needed to be released *Godward*, not *inward*. This painful season was not for complaining about what I was losing; it was a time for singing praises with all the strength of the life remaining in me.

I had to rise above my complaining that people were forgetting me. It was time to rejoice in God's promise: "I will never leave thee, nor forsake thee" (Hebrews 13:5).

If we must make a choice between the presence and comfort of people or the presence and comfort of God, the choice is not difficult. Always choose the Eternal One. I did, and I have found it to be a wise choice. His inner presence brings glorious deliverance from depression.

During this lonely season I have discovered that I could encourage myself in God to such an extent that I received strength to endure extreme suffering and pain that filled my life. If I fill my mind with the Word of God, I can't be depressed, for all that God is, has done, and has become lifts me out of a depressed state and into a praise state. I have widely taught on praise in my last years of ministry, and now, during this time, I have a good opportunity to put it into practice. You cannot praise and remain depressed.

"Why am I able to exercise my faith for my salvation but not for healing?"

Often when my son-in-law Norbert Senftleben is praying for me, he likes to remind me of the glorious truth that Christ bore all of my pain in His body on the cross of Calvary. The prophet Isaiah adds that Jesus took all our sicknesses as well as our pain. Since Jesus bore it all, I need not bear any of it. Our Savior is a healing Lord by virtue of His substitutionary work.

This reality raises the painful question: "Why is it that I can exercise faith for salvation but not for my healing, since both were purchased at the same time?" I don't know. I have searched diligently for this answer, but it has eluded me so far.

For years I have proclaimed the finished work of Jesus at Calvary. I have preached it, taught it, written books about it, and entered into singing about it. Yet, at this juncture, I must admit that I have succeeded in appropriating only a portion of the provision Jesus purchased for me. The fault is not God's. It is quite obviously mine! This is embarrassing to me.

It seems that God gives us the gift of faith for salvation. Perhaps the faith needed for healing is produced by ourselves. I have heard it preached that since divine healing is in the atonement, as is salvation, then it should be just as easy to get hold of it as salvation. While that preaches well, it doesn't practice well.

I have been a man of faith, have lived by faith, taught faith, and have faith for financial needs, but finding sufficient faith in my spirit for my own healing has proven to be impossible. I do not understand this. I only admit it. Maybe God doesn't give the measure of faith for healing to everyone as He has given the gift of faith for salvation. I don't know. I just know that it is marvelous when it comes, and I praise Him for the testimonies I hear of the saving and healing faith of Jesus.

"How should I respond to people who try to get me to try 'cures' they hear about?"

I have been given so many "cures" for cancer. Some of them came in little bottles, and some came with electric motors. Some had batteries and things that you plugged in under your wrist. I have been given all kinds of instant cure-alls for my condition.

I took one of them to the doctor and told him about all the things I was receiving. "Will these work?" I asked him.

He simply replied, "If you believe in them. But I think you're better off to believe in your God!"

Telling a sick man that some doctor up in Canada has the cure for his illness is very unfair. It's not true, but the man who is desperately seeking for answers can become so confused by so many "remedies" being thrown his way. I think that is very hurtful...very hurtful.

Put your trust in the medical professionals to whom you have entrusted your care and in your heavenly Physician, Jesus Christ.

"How can I help my loved ones and friends to face this positively with me?"

This is a difficult question. When you see the hurt in their eyes, the grief, the fear, and the anxiety your sickness has produced in them, you reach out to grasp for words, but they don't seem to come. We can only tell them that we are convinced the Lord is on the throne and that He is doing things well. The same Lord who has used me to bless them will use others to bless them after I am gone. I have tried to turn their attention to the Lord Jesus Christ and His glorious promises. I have found that if they can see my faith rather than my fear, then their own personal grief is handled nicely, too.

LEAVING A LEGACY~*For doing all the good things you do, for being all the good things you are, for being one of those people, thank you.*

Speak positively to them when they come to visit. Let them see your faith, not your fears. Hold them up in prayer, for as they pray for you, you pray for them. Let them see that you are not facing death with fear; therefore, they can face your death fearlessly. Turn them to the Word of God, and help them to realize that a death sentence was pronounced on us at the time of our birth. God has been wonderful to let us live in peace all these years.

Involve them with you in your times of praise and thanksgiving to God. Communicate with them openly about your process of moving from negative thinking to positive thinking. Rehearse the goodness of God and His never-failing promises with them. Involve them as much as possible in this journey of grace that you are taking so that they do not feel left out or left behind. Encourage them in the Lord just as you have learned to encourage yourself in the Lord.

Entrust them to God—He is their heavenly Father and will surround them with His presence and His provision, just as He has surrounded you.

TRUSTING GOD FOR THE ANSWERS

I have fought these questions—and others—on my painful journey, for I am a human being seeking for answers that God has chosen to conceal—not to reveal. I am sufficiently childlike to ask "Why?" even though I remember how aggravating my children's "Why?" used to get. Yes, I remember in my frustration giving them an emphasized "Because!" I think I have heard that same answer from God sometimes. While it doesn't satisfy my curiosity, even that enigmatic answer is welcome as it assures me that God is listening.

And the tyrannical question remains: *why?* There will not always be an answer to such questions. But there is a way to deal with these questions when they surface: submit your questions to worship. I have learned to do that in my illness, and I want to help you learn to do that in my later chapter called "Exhorting Myself." If you will focus your attention on worshiping Christ, the cares and problems of this temporary life on earth will be placed where they belong—under the covering of praise.

1. Cornwall, *The Secret of Personal Prayer*, 119–120.
2. Ibid., 121.
3. Ibid., 125.
4. Ibid., 126.
5. Judson Cornwall, *David Worshiped With a Fervent Faith* (Shippensburg, PA: Destiny Image Publishers, 1993).
6. Ibid., 159.

KEY PRINCIPLE

Enduring pain—physical, emotional, or spiritual—can help develop in us the character of Christ.

Consider it all joy, my brethren, when you encounter various trials, knowing that the testing of your faith produces endurance. And let endurance have its perfect result, that you may be perfect and complete, lacking in nothing.

—JAMES 1:2–4, NAS

CHAPTER 5

Enduring Pain

> For I reckon that the sufferings of this present
> time are not worthy to be compared with the
> glory which shall be revealed in us.
>
> —ROMANS 8:18

I fear that the person who declared that pain is a blessing has not endured very much pain. Still, I understand the concept that pain is an alarm system to alert us to the fact that something is wrong. Personally, I have felt that alarm system scream like an air raid siren in my body.

If, indeed, it is true that pain is a blessing, then I am a very blessed man. I am also a person with an acute awareness that something is wrong—very wrong.

ACCEPTING THE MEDICAL SOLUTION

Although I was resting at home, and relatively comfortable, the pain persisted. The doctor's answer for my pain levels at the hospital was to prescribe morphine. I was unhappy with that decision because I visualized myself being hooked on the drug and living with a greatly reduced mental sharpness. I was relieved to find out that administering the drug was not left up to me. The hospice group to which I had been assigned would be in charge of administering all my medication.

I had been completely ignorant about the ministry of hospice groups. Fundamentally, hospice is assigned to a dying patient to guide him or her through the last days of life and to give assistance to the family. Through hospice services, I have a registered nurse assigned to me who doles out my medication twice a week. She also acts as a liaison between the doctor and me. I have a bathing nurse who comes to my house three times a week to help me bathe and to make my bed. A counselor comes on a monthly basis to help me with any emotional problems that may be bothering me. They even have a visiting pastor available.

These are wonderful services all provided through hospice. I feel very cradled in arms of love and care, and my wife has the security of knowing these helpers can be summoned day or night by a phone call. This particular hospice is a Catholic organization, and my workers all profess a genuine personal relationship with Jesus Christ. We have prayer together when they come to serve me. Hallelujah!

Although my medication was being controlled and administered by a trained professional who is answerable to the doctor, I was still uncomfortable in having to take morphine pills. My nurse didn't argue with me. She simply said, "The choice is yours—pain or pills." It wasn't long before I realized that I could not function with high pain levels, so I submitted to "low doses" of morphine, though still uncomfortable with my decision.

Norbert, my son-in-law, comes almost every day after work to pray for me. His demonstrated love has moved him from a relationship of son-in-law to the son-I-love.

He is the son I never had. In one of our evening prayer meetings, he reminded me that God created the plants from which we get morphine. "It shouldn't be so wrong to partake as needed of what God has provided," he said.

As is often the case, his words made sense to me, which eased my discomfort with my decision to submit to the medication. With every visit by my hospice nurse, Kathleen, came her plea to increase my dosage. I was very reluctant to give in, but little by little, I surrendered to her. I still do not take enough to completely kill the pain, but it is dulled sufficiently to allow me to function.

I really don't understand all the medication I take. About a dozen pills in the morning and another dozen at night are doled out to me. Sometimes I shudder at the amount of medication it takes to keep me going these days. I was blessed with such good strength for so many years. I would often boast that I didn't even take four aspirin tablets a year. Oh, how God must laugh at the boastings of our youth.

LEAVING A LEGACY ~ *May the Lord gently touch you with His awesome power.*

The ministry of the hospice group is to the dying. It is not too unusual for a new client of theirs to be dead within a week. I'm still alive after nearly three years. Fearing that I may be dropped from their care program, I have discussed my dilemma with my hospice nurse and also with the counselor.

They told me that my case has regularly been discussed at headquarters, and that they are going to continue to minister to me, with the realization that I am still a very sick man. They expect me to die, and, of course, I agree with them.

The issue is, *when* will I die? Obviously, it is not in the time frame the doctors had set. I have to agree with the psalmist who declared, "My times are in thy hand"

(Psalm 31:15). I am now on God's time schedule, and He is not sharing His timing with me right now. My inability to read God's timetable is also embarrassing to me.

Addressing Emotional and Spiritual Pain

The physical pain is not the only pain I have to endure. When I look into the eyes of my precious wife and see the pain and anxiety that often distress her, I hurt with her. For the nearly sixty years of our marriage, I have been the strength upon which she could lean. Now I must lean on her. At a time in life when she should be allowed to sit back in her lounge chair and play with her great-grandchildren, she is busy caring for me. This pains me.

If I need anything, she has to get it for me. If I need to go anywhere, she must drive me, for my driving privileges were revoked when I began taking morphine. This too is painful for a man with an independent spirit.

In the mercies of God, I now have sufficient strength to be up at least for the morning hours, but my wife has to help me dress. She never complains, but it is a source of inner pain to have to lean on her for such mundane things.

The Lord has been a source of strength and peace to her through this difficult process. She has learned much about this whole process of death and dying that will be helpful to the many other spouses who are facing such an experience. When someone asked her to express what she has learned, her answer gave simple advice that is profoundly important to understand. "I was raised on a farm with a very, very spiritual mother," she responded, "and she always said, 'If the Lord wants to take them, you let them go.'" Then my wife continued by explaining how she had lived out this advice from her mother. "So, every day," she explained, "I just have to say, 'Lord, I have him one more day. Now Your will be done. Help me to do the things that are important today, because I don't know how many more I will have with him.'"

She explained that she has to determine hour by hour what she can do for me. On some days my pain is worse; on others I can move around a little more. So she just asks the Lord for His grace, His will, His mercy, and His strength.

That's good advice to follow for anyone—whether you have a sick spouse or not.

Spiritual pain? Yes! When there are special services at the church that I cannot attend for lack of strength, I am pained in my spirit. When I have to miss family gatherings and cause my wife to miss them, I am pained in my soul. When I do make the effort to go to church on Sunday morning and well-meaning friends hug me enthusiastically, I am pained in my body. At first I used to verbalize these pains, but I discovered that I was merely transferring my pain to others without healing my own pain. I had to learn to suffer with my mouth closed.

When I first found ample strength to go to church on Sunday morning, I misunderstood the standard question people asked: "How are you?" They really aren't interested in a medical report. They are being polite. I found that a simple response of "I am better" was sufficient. They don't ask whether I mean better than yesterday or better than tomorrow. "Better" with a smile and a polite "thank you" satisfies both them and me. It is a grace-filled answer that blesses both of us.

ASSENTING TO A BIBLICAL PATTERN

I have found that enduring pain, whether physical, emotional, or spiritual, must often be done in silence. It is a lonely vigil, but one that the Savior understands and shares with you. And endurance itself is touted in Scripture as a virtuous character trait. The apostle Paul instructed Timothy: "Thou therefore endure hardness, as a good soldier of Jesus Christ" (2 Timothy 2:3). And again, Paul told Timothy: "But watch thou in all things, endure afflictions…" (2 Timothy 4:5).

Even Christ had to submit to this aspect of obedience, for the writer to the Hebrews declares:

> Looking unto Jesus the author and finisher of our faith; who for the joy that was set before him *endured* the cross, despising the shame, and is set down at the right hand of the throne of God. For consider him that *endured* such contradiction of sinners against himself, lest ye be wearied and faint in your minds.
> —HEBREWS 12:2–3, EMPHASIS ADDED

It is James who describes the benefit of patience (also translated "endurance") in trials:

> Consider it all joy, my brethren, when you encounter various trials, knowing that the testing of your faith produces endurance. And let endurance have its perfect result, that you may be perfect and complete, lacking in nothing.
> —JAMES 1:2–4, NAS

I am not justifying my illness as a means for my perfection. Yet it seems the principle of endurance can be applied to any affliction we bear.

PLANNING IN RETROSPECT

What should we have done differently? By planning in retrospect, it's possible that the lessons we have learned can be helpful to you when you are facing similar decisions. No doubt there are other things that should be done in preparation for a major illness, but some of the suggestions below may be helpful to you.

Putting things in order

When given the doctor's prognosis, we acted in complete honesty. I made sure that my will and testament was in order. I arranged for the disposal of much of my property. Given the present circumstances, my pastor brother, Jim, stepped in and said that nothing could be taken before my death. What wisdom that was. I have needed the use of some of that property during these two years that have passed since my death sentence was pronounced, and I continue to need it for the time remaining.

Several years ago, I was given an unusually large honorarium from a church where my ministry had been particularly blessed of the Lord. When my wife and I discussed what to do with these unexpected funds, we felt it might be wise for us to go ahead and purchase prepaid funeral plans. We went to a local mortuary that had been highly recommended to me by my brother Jim and purchased the funeral plan in full. We purchased our caskets and arranged the service we wanted, naming our pallbearers and so forth. We purchased the burial plot and bought the headstones. Our names were inscribed on the headstones with the dates of our birth, and the stones were placed on the burial site. We felt this would be a blessing to the family, and it has been a relaxing blessing to us. Now that I am living under a death sentence, I'm so pleased that these arrangements have been made.

Living Longer Than Expected

All this to say that as much as lies within me, I "had my ducks in a row," as the old saying goes. As I have shared, my family had come to my bedside with loving respect, and we exchanged hugs and kisses on repeated occasions. Why couldn't I just die? I wanted to go. I was ready to go. The doctors said that I was on my way out. What was hindering the process? This delay was embarrassing me.

Some people believe that a strong-willed person can determinedly "will" the time of his or her death. Don't you believe it! I have a very strong will, but when it came up against the will of God in this regard, it proved to be extremely puny. Aside from a cowardly act of suicide, no one can produce his or her death by willing it. Our times are in God's hands whether we like it or not.

LEAVING A LEGACY~May you be surrounded with heavenly care and ministry in your agony of pain.

Yet I still ask, "Why can't I die?" The doctors predicted my death, I have prepared for it, my wife submitted to its immediacy, and my children say they have released me to it. What's holding up the parade?

When King Cyrus granted Ezra permission to return to Jerusalem to rebuild the temple, the heathen king gave him all the vessels of gold that Nebuchadnezzar had stolen from the temple before it was destroyed years earlier. In addition to this, Ezra was given additional gold and silver, which made the little group of Jews who returned to Jerusalem under Ezra's leadership a logical prey to thieves. Ezra reports:

> For I was *ashamed* to require of the king a band of soldiers and horsemen to help us against the enemy in the way: because we had spoken unto the king, saying, The hand of our God is upon all them for good that seek him; but his power and his wrath is against all them that forsake him.
> —EZRA 8:22, EMPHASIS ADDED

Ezra had bragged on God. Now he was embarrassed to ask a heathen king for help. He called his returning companions to join him in fasting and entreating God for His protection against attack during the journey, and they didn't lose an ounce of gold on the trip to Jerusalem.

Applying this passage to my own situation may be stretching the metaphor, but for years I had relied on God for my physical well-being. Now that I had put myself into the hands of doctors, everything seemed to turn out wrong. I do not say this to fault the doctors, but to fault myself.

Why was I so quick to accept their death sentence? Was it the pain? Maybe. Was it the medication they gave me at the hospital? Perhaps. Was I simply too tired of the struggle to keep going? I don't know. I only know for sure that I completely embraced the report that my death was near, and I gave in to it.

Almost two years ago, I went into the hospital to get some relief from the pain I was experiencing, expecting the problem to be quite treatable by the doctors. I came out five days later fully embracing the doctor's death sentence. His prognosis has proven to be very inaccurate. It is embarrassing to me, for my family and I proclaimed this death sentence as though God had spoken it to us by angels. This is far from the truth. Man, not God, said I was dying. But I believed it, and that has utterly embarrassed me.

Instead of hearing what trained men had to say, I needed to hear what *God* had to say about my physical condition. I needed a word of prophecy—and shortly after receiving the doctor's prognosis, God obliged me. He sent my dear sister to me to give me prophetic understanding I desperately needed.

KEY PRINCIPLE

There are numerous ways we can be
fruitful in ministry in our
desire to please God.

If thou put the brethren in remembrance of these things, thou shalt be a good minister of Jesus Christ, nourished up in the words of faith and of good doctrine, whereunto thou hast attained.

—1 TIMOTHY 4:6

CHAPTER 6

Extended Ministry

Now I want you to know, brethren, that my circumstances have turned out for the greater
progress of the gospel...
—PHILIPPIANS 1:12, NAS

A life-debilitating illness such as cancer can seem to
destroy all evidence of a useful life and make one
feel "put out to pasture." Not only did I have to
learn to accept my death sentence, but I also had to learn
to live with it—and for much longer than I had anticipated.
Yet was I really *living*, or was I merely breathing in this
broken-down shell of a body until I drew my final breath?

In this chapter I want to explore these questions and
others that people face when they are put on the sidelines
by a debilitating illness. I want you to discover, as I have,
that there is still a purpose for you being alive, that God,
your loving heavenly Father, has work for you to do even
from a bed of illness. May you discover the joy of being
"redirected" by the Lord into paths of ministry you never

anticipated. If your desire is to please God, then there are many ways that you can do this. Continue reading to see how God has directed me in ministry.

ENJOYING FAMILY IN A NEW WAY

My only sister, Iverna Tompkins, travels widely in a prophetic-teaching ministry. Her days at home are few and busy. Yet she took time off to be with me and share her love. We have been very close through the years. One particular day, shortly after I had come home to die, she leaned herself across the foot of my bed as loving affection was flowing comfortably between us.

"Judson," she said softly, "I really don't believe your ministry has been completed. I believe that God wants to use you in your home. I feel that your wife, children, grandchildren, and great-grandchildren need you."

What could I say? When Iverna speaks in a prophetic mode, her accuracy is amazing. Yet, it would be natural in this circumstance to wonder: *Was God speaking through her, or was the heart of a sister trying to sidestep the harsh reality that her beloved brother, the one man in her life, was dying?*

I was lying there with breathing tubes in my nose and with barely enough strength to take care of my toilet duties, and my sister was commanding me to continue to live—and minister. There was nothing to do but to wait and see. I was willing to have my death date postponed, but there was nothing I could do to delay it.

Time seems to have proven my sister's prophetic voice to be accurate once again. I have not only had an increased ministry to my family, but also I have come into a new intimacy with my wife. My entire extended family has paid quite a price for my ministry through the years, for I was frequently away for several consecutive weeks at a time. Often when I did arrive home, I had a mountain of correspondence to care for, schedules to fine-tune, and a weary body that needed to rest. It had gotten to the point that when my daughters telephoned me, they apologized for doing so.

This unavailability to my family was a sacrifice made "in the name of God." I was busy fulfilling my calling to the ministry, and my family accepted this priority in my life. All of my family had learned to respect what I felt was a divine calling, except for my little dog. He wildly protested every time I left on another assignment "for God," and there was simply no way to comfort or reassure him that I would return.

My sickness erased all my excuses for living in a virtual social vacuum, separated from my family. No one felt the need to apologize for "taking my time" to be with me. Family members felt free to sit on the foot of my bed or on a chair and visit with me as long as they desired.

After the first few visits, their talk was no longer just "spiritual" talk. I found that I enjoyed hearing my great-grandchildren tell me about school. My daughters began to share more openly with Daddy, and even my wife and I came into a more honest communication with each other. I found that impending death erases many false barriers we build up over the course of the years.

Encountering Grace for Brokenness

While I was still confined to bed with restricted breathing and extreme weakness, David, the only son of my middle daughter, Jeannie, flew to my bedside from Atlanta. He brought his estranged wife, Lori, and their son, Jon Jon, with him. They came to pay last respects to Grandpa Cornwall. I believe their visit surprised me the most of anyone who had come to see me.

The pressure of being in the ministry had succeeded in breaking up their marriage. This, as you have observed, is a favorite trick of the devil.

That they were willing to come together to see their dying grandpa was a minor miracle in its own right, but that's what they did. To our amazement, their little three-year-old boy crawled up from the foot of the bed, laid his head on my shoulder, and went sound asleep.

Why? Did Jon Jon feel the peace in the room, or did God know what this could do to the parents' hearts? I don't have a clue. I know only that this incident played a major role in causing this couple to take another look at their lives and remarry each other. What a beautiful union it has become.

A few months after my grandson and his wife were reunited, I sat straight up in bed after being in a sound sleep and announced that I was bringing David and his family to Phoenix to live. I got the wheels turning, and in far less time than I thought possible, we were able to purchase a house for them just about a block from his mother's house.

Everything fell into place quickly for them, and it wasn't long before they moved in. What a blessing this family has become. Their house is very commodious for family gatherings, and we have already had a family feast there. The wedding of his mother took place in his backyard, but more of that later.

Would this couple's marriage have been salvaged if I had gone home to glory as rapidly as the doctors predicted? I don't know. I just know that God wanted to use me as the catalyst to rescue a couple to whom God had imparted a gift of hospitality. It has been worth the extra pain I have had to endure to remain here, for nothing is more sacred to God than a Christian marriage. He hates to see a marriage break apart, but He rejoices greatly to see one get healed.

ENTREATING PERSONAL INTIMACY

Their marriage is not the only marriage that has come to health during this time. I feel that my own marriage has been given an injection of new life. Eleanor and I have been blessed with a deep love for one another. I fear that during the years, I have taken Eleanor's love and commitment to me for granted. In retrospect, I realize that Eleanor has had to stand in line behind my "ministry," my writing schedule that has been very heavy, and my response to the needs of others. God helped preserve this marriage by impressing on Eleanor that I was not too different from a chief executive who had worldwide responsibilities.

> LEAVING A LEGACY~*I thank God for you and the godly imprint you have helped to form in my life.*

I tried to give my wife some priority time when I was home, but most of it was spent within the boundaries of our home. I didn't want to go out for anything. I had all the restaurant food I could handle while out on the road.

If I had all the complaints she has offered through the years together on paper, it wouldn't fill a single page. She has done her suffering in silence. Sadly, I was so wrapped up in my expanding ministry that I failed to recognize her loneliness.

When I was a young pastor, I would often bring the problems of the church to bed with me. One night while I lay on my back worrying about something, she put her cold little feet on my thigh and said, "Kick the saints out of bed. This is your wife in bed with you." For years, she didn't have me in the bed to startle with cold feet. She had to endure weeks, and sometime months, of being alone.

Oh, I phoned her every night when I was in America and every week when I was out of the country, but a five- or ten-minute phone call isn't quite the same as a long personal conversation. In addition to this weakness in communication, I usually phoned her when I got back to my room. I was either exhausted or still euphoric with the anointing of the evening. Neither mood was conducive to discussing what she was facing—a broken washing machine or a problem with the car, or deeper issues like personal loneliness.

Eleanor, in wisdom, recognized this, so she saved these matters to discuss with me when I arrived home. My brief time home before going out on my next assignment was often consumed with problem solving. I had little time to play.

Now, that is all behind me. I am home perpetually. Everything I do is a team effort with Eleanor. We eat all our meals together. I am so thankful that not only is she a great cook, but also that she enjoys the kitchen. She has become my "legs" as she carries items for me from my lounge chair here in the family room to the office attached to our house where my secretary works. She has to take me wherever I need to go, and she is responsible for all the shopping.

Her kind, sweet way of ministering to my continual needs during this time has been a blessing to me. I have done my best to be a "good patient," and I hope her comment to another person recently indicates that I have been partially successful. My sweet wife said that I have been far more sympathetic now than earlier, and very patient, not complaining or whining. "He's done a lot of quiet praying to himself," she said, "and been very gracious, which I didn't think was possible because he was so active, and such a go-getter, and so full of vigor. This has to be a work of grace in his life that he allowed the Lord to do. He didn't have that before." How grateful I am for this work of grace the Lord has done in my life. This has been a wonderful time with my wife.

We are both living out our "golden" years. We laughingly say that it takes the two of us to make one person. What one cannot remember the other one generally can. We now communicate on little things as a matter of survival. The marriage ceremony says, "The two shall become one flesh," but the simple recitation of those words over a couple cannot produce such oneness. It takes a heap of living to do this. We are rediscovering what being together is all about—and we are enjoying it very much in spite of the pain and sickness.

In fairness, I must admit that my marriage has not been threatened by my demanding lifestyle. Eleanor and I hold fast to the vows that we took when we stood in front of my father in Vallejo, California, in June of 1943. What was threatened in our marriage was the joy of being a team. Constant separation of life duties required us to live "alone." Since receiving my death sentence, we are living together in a marital oneness that neither of us would have wanted to miss—it is the wonder of exhilarating love.

I have shared only a few ways the prophetic word God gave my sister, Iverna, has been fulfilled during this time regarding my family relationships. And these blessings are still unfolding—so much to praise God for that I would have missed without this unexpected "timing" of my journey.

If you are set aside from what you believed to be your ministry by a debilitating illness, seek the Lord's wisdom to help you discover new ways of extended ministry opportunities that you can do now. Begin with your family; allow God to birth new ministry to them. God has a purpose for your life—one for your life right now! Trust Him to lead you into it.

Ministry Opportunities
in the Body of Christ

As wonderful as the love of family has become, this isn't all that has been gained through the unpredicted extension of my life. There are other facets of extended ministry developing as well, in spite of the difficulties of my illness.

During more than six decades of ministry, I have traveled thousands of miles to minister to people. It seemed necessary at the time. Leaders felt I had the ministry that was needed, and the "needy" ones were in a faraway country.

Of course, my traveling days are now history. At present, it almost saps my energies completely just to go to church on Sunday mornings, and I live less than five miles from the church. It should be patently obvious, then, that I could not survive a flight to Asia, Africa, South America, or even to the East Coast.

According to the Scriptures, God's ways are not our ways (Isaiah 55:8). At times they even seem devious to us. Since I cannot go to the people to extend my ministry to the needy, God arranges for them to come to me to receive the life He has given me to share with them.

Wouldn't it have been wonderful if the apostle Paul had been given access to our modern forms of communication? How he would have loved a fax machine, a telephone, a computer, and e-mail. He had none of these, but I have all of them, and they all are operative in the extension of the ministry God wants to flow through me.

"Accepting" Appointments

I had barely been weaned from the oxygen tubes and was in my study when the fax machine began to receive a message. It was from a pastor's wife saying that her husband was flying home from another country by way of Phoenix,

80

and she was flying from their home in another state to meet him here. Andy (not his real name) wanted the two of them to meet with me. She acknowledged her awareness of my illness, but she said their need was urgent and that they wouldn't take much of my time.

I didn't have the strength for even a pleasant visit with them, much less a counseling session that would be worth their trouble to fly all the way to Phoenix. But I wasn't being given an option; I had not been asked for an appointment—I had simply been informed of their coming. Besides, there wasn't enough time to contact her. They were conveniently arriving in Phoenix the day I received the fax.

I had previously been involved with this couple from the time they first entered the ministry. I had walked them through some hard places both in their ministry and in their marriage. They were very successful in their ministry, taking a struggling congregation of less than one hundred members and developing the church into a congregation of more than two thousand people. I doubted that the problem was in the church, so I assumed it must lie in their marriage.

When their rental car pulled up in front of the house, I sent up a desperate last minute prayer for strength and met them in my study. I was delighted to share renewed fellowship with them. However, in my extreme weakness, I was not completely cognizant of everything I was telling them. We talked for about an hour, and then with the little strength I had left, I laid hands on them and prayed for them.

They graciously left just before I collapsed, and I didn't hear from either of them for many weeks. When I did finally receive word, Rev. Andy said our time together was a life-changing experience for them. He declared that my prayers were prophetic and said my prayer over him gave him needed guidance for both the church and for their personal lives.

You could have fooled me. I was unaware of any blessing I had been to them. I knew only exhaustion and pain, but God used me in spite of myself—making use even of my fax machine to establish His sovereign "appointment." Perhaps I was experiencing in a new dimension the scriptural promise that His strength will be made perfect in my weakness (2 Corinthians 12:9).

Have you considered what ministry you could have by using modern technology available at your fingertips—even if you are bedridden?

ACCESSIBILITY BY PHONE

Choosing an example of ministry by telephone is not difficult, for it happens so frequently. I think of a special couple in my life who have been prayer partners with me for many years. They are now retired and have moved to a different area to live where they know very few persons. They have no children.

I received a tearful phone call from Agnes (not her real name) saying that her husband seemed to have lost control of his thinking. He now viewed her as a vile woman who was demonized, and he often shouted at her while flaying his arms wildly, trying to cast the demons out of her. This behavior was completely out of character for him. He had been a gentle, loving, and almost passive person for years. Yet his wife was now afraid of him.

The doctors didn't have a clue as to what could be wrong with the man, so they just medicated him while they prepared to send him to a specialist. As his wife shared her sad story with me, my heart was first filled with pity for her and then moved to anger against the devil. As we talked, I begin to plead the blood of Jesus over her and commanded this troubling, afflicting spirit to leave their house.

She later told me that my prayer marked the end to his problem. Since then, her husband has not experienced another outburst. In fact, his wife told me that he was back to his old, lovable self again.

I couldn't go to Agnes to minister to this couple's need, for we are separated by over two thousand miles. But it is simply a fact that there is no distance in prayer. Hallelujah! It is wonderful to know that, sick or not, God can still get glory from my life.

ACTIVATING MINISTRY BY MAIL

E-mail is the chosen form of communication for many people. It is fast, cheap, and very informal. I get my share of e-mails daily, and many of them ask for guidance or advice in life's problems. I am so grateful to God for the many, many times He has flowed His life through me, giving me inspiration for what to write.

Many of these inquiries come from young pastors of small churches. They have no denominational ties with leadership to give them guidance. And they seem to feel quite comfortable in pouring out their perplexities in a nonthreatening e-mail. I am often the person to whom they bear their heart. In spite of living under a death sentence, I can still share living truths with them that encourage, comfort, or guide.

While citing the fruitful use of the various forms of modern communication, I dare not negate the old "snail mail" form of letter writing. It is slower and much more expensive, but many persons in my age bracket are not computer literate and must rely on pen and paper. The mail carrier brings me letters on a daily basis, and some of them offer opportunities for ministry. Some writers have needs, while other correspondents are inviting me to join them in rejoicing over victories won. These are my favorite letters.

ACKNOWLEDGING THE POWER OF PRAYER

Perhaps the most powerful ministry in which I am involved daily is the ministry of prayer. I not only have my private, personal prayer time as I begin each new morning, but I am also involved in our "threefold cord" prayer channel each evening. There is a powerful little verse in the Book of Ecclesiastes that declares that a threefold cord is not easily broken (Ecclesiastes 4:12).

I have already mentioned that my son-in-law Norbert stops by each evening after work to join with Eleanor and me for a season of prayer. It is a special time of earnestly worshiping the Lord and laying our petitions before Him. We feel that our united prayers are more powerful than our private prayers.

At times, these prayers are mostly praise and rejoicing before the Lord. There are other times, however, when a strong spirit of intercession grips us, and we plead with God in great earnest for a specific need or problem. Only eternity will reveal everything we have accomplished, but we have seen some immediate answers, and that encourages us.

Other opportunities for prayer ministry have presented themselves as I have sensitized myself to opportunities to minister to the people who come regularly to our home. I have already mentioned that I pray for my nurses every time they come to minister to me. At times, they have wept as I prayed over them. Other times, they joyfully enter into a hearty "Amen!" and squeeze my hand gratefully. A couple of them have admitted that this is a "first" for them.

I occasionally have to remind myself that I am not "out of the ministry" simply because I am no longer walking through airports. I just have to recognize the ministry opportunities that present themselves in various ways in my home. This reality requires that I be spiritually ready at all times. That is the reason my first ministry must be ministry to myself.

ACQUIESCING THE PULPIT MINISTRY

I continued to gain more strength week after week. For a while, I thought that God was healing me, but, so far, this has not proven to be true. However, I found that I could function without the oxygen tubes. Freedom from those tubes was like a gift from heaven.

Feeling stronger, I thought that I could probably do some pulpit ministry again, so I accepted the invitation from my oldest daughter, Dorothy, and her husband to speak at their church on a Sunday morning. I preached from a comfortable chair with pillows to prop me up. All went well, but the physical toll it took made me realize that I did not have sufficient strength for public ministry. And I haven't preached anywhere since then.

Further, I have concluded, as I have watched the many preachers God has available to Him on television, that I am no longer needed in the pulpit. I believe that there comes a time when it is proper to step down and let the younger generation carry the ministry burden for the churches. Furthermore, this is a very different generation from the one in which I was reared. I fear that my preaching could be quite "dated" and out of step with today's world. Of course, the gospel is never out of date, but the application of gospel truth does have to adjust to the audience.

These conclusions don't mean that I can't effectively minister to the needs of people. They simply give credence to reasons for allowing God to readjust my ministry. And, as I have discussed, I have found precious ministry apart from the pulpit.

ACCEPTING MORE MINISTRY FROM HOME

I received an e-mail from Ruth Versaw, the head of a very successful lending library for the blind in Oklahoma. I have been active with this library for several years, purchasing new tapes for them and making tapes of my teaching ministry available to them. In her e-mail, expressing her thanks for some more tapes we had sent to her, Ruth remarked that the blind would be very pleased to hear my actual voice narrate on tape as author of many books in their library, instead of someone else's voice doing the narration.

LEAVING A LEGACY~Your life of preaching and encouragement meant so much to us at a very significant time in our lives. You are known to our friends as our "daddy in the Lord."

Ruth gave me some amazing statistics about how many blind persons are living in our nation. I was equally amazed at how many of these folks were borrowing tapes from her lending library. When I read her note, I felt an inner prompting of the Holy Spirit to make myself available to record the reading of some of my books for the library.

During my high school days, I had worked part time with a blind piano tuner. He hired me to be his "eyes" whenever he came to work in our vicinity. Through this relationship, I gained a tremendous respect for blind persons and their ability to cope with and compensate for their handicap. An enduring compassion for the blind made me anxious now to do whatever I could to help them.

I also have some commercial radio experience, and a few years ago, I had developed a small recording studio in a corner of my office for another project involving recording my reading of the Scriptures. So I was equipped to do the job with no financial outlay, beyond the cost of the tapes. It is probably good that I didn't know how many tapes I would need, however, or I might have backed out of the operation. But I discovered again in this project the truth of what I had learned earlier in my ministry: God underwrites any program that He ordains.

When I realized that I had the time, the equipment, the expertise, and the invitation to proceed, I could find no reason to refuse entering into this wonderful new avenue of ministry to meet the needs of precious blind people. Recording the reading of the first book went very slowly, but I soon got up to speed. Originally, I committed myself to reading only two or three books, but the enthusiastic response of the blind, being able to actually hear the author narrate his own book to them, soon had me committing to recording more of my books.

Although I have never met Ruth, I can say with certainty that she is an amazing motivator. With regularity, she sent glowing excerpts from letters she received from blind recipients of the tapes. I was reminded that we, who have our sight, forget what the blind miss in everyday living.

I found that I could muster up enough energy to read aloud about an hour a day. I have now read all of the books I have written, more than forty in all, and I am now reading the writings of other authors.

My limited understanding regarding my physical situation is that the cancer has produced some small, and some not so small, tumors in my body cavity. The pain level is generated according to where these tumors are active. I would not have survived if these tumors were growing on a vital organ in my body. Apparently, they are developing in nonlethal areas, which, however, does not make them less painful.

Accounting for Ministry Overflow

The blind are not the only beneficiaries of these recorded readings. I was personally deeply blessed myself by reading these truths again. Years have passed since I wrote some of my books. It was spiritually refreshing for me to hear what the Spirit of God was saying to and through me in those writings. I pray that I will never get so anxious to hear a "new" revelation from God that I lose the thrill of what He has already taught me.

God consistently teaches us by proceeding from the known to the unknown. Just as learning the alphabet precedes learning how to write, so first principles will always precede "the deep things of God," as Paul expressed it (1 Corinthians 2:10). I dare not forget what God taught me in the early years, for this becomes the platform from which fresh truth can be shared.

And the overflow of this ministry to the blind continues. Two book publishers are looking into the financial feasibility of making these readings available to the public. With so many persons spending time in commuting to and from work on a daily basis, there is a growing market for audio books. And as the word has spread that I have made these recordings, we have received many requests for copies. It seems the Lord was again exercising His sovereignty in having me make these tapes at this time. He seems to enjoy being at the head of the "learning curve."

I have been asked why I don't make these tapes available to the public myself. People who ask that question are simply unaware of what such a production would require. Besides the need to resolve copyright issues, I have neither the finances nor the facilities to venture into such a project. It needs to be accomplished by someone who has considerable financial resources and is otherwise equipped for the task. One person alone seldom carries out the work of the Lord. God prefers teamwork to solo performances. As Paul expressed it, "I have planted, Apollos watered; but God gave the increase" (1 Corinthians 3:6). I am waiting for the teamwork concept to expedite this project, and for God to give increase as well.

As I have watched other avenues of ministry dry up because I could not physically continue to perform them, I may also see the ministry of reading to the blind come to an end. It is satisfying to know, however, that other avenues of ministry are opening as a result and can, in turn, blossom for a season.

Who says I don't have a ministry? Compared to speaking to vast audiences, the ministry for which I presently have strength to be accountable is small, personal, and private. It will not go unrewarded, for God promises that what He sees in secret He will reward openly (Matthew 6:4). Praise His name!

I trust that I have successfully whetted your appetite to be involved in extended ministry from your bedside. There are so many people who need to be ministered to and so many available ways to touch their lives with God's compassion and love from your home. Ask God to reveal your ministry to you, and then be willing to get involved and to stay involved in service to your Lord.

When someone asked my assistant, Terri, to tell him why she believes I've lived so much longer than the doctors said I would, she gave this response: "He's done so much—he's written, read for audio books, and it's just like a second ministry to him. There's a purpose that he's still here." I'm so glad I discovered my purpose for this season of my life. I'm praying that you will also discover your purpose for this time.

KEY PRINCIPLE

Sometimes we will have to encourage
ourselves in the Lord.

Furthermore then we beseech you, brethren, and exhort you by the Lord Jesus, that as ye have received of us how ye ought to walk and to please God, so ye would abound more and more.

—1 THESSALONIANS 4:1

CHAPTER 7

Exhorting Myself

Bless the LORD, O my soul: and all that is
within me, bless his holy name.

—PSALM 103:1

Throughout my ministry, I have enjoyed preaching
and teaching from the apostle Paul's great theo-
logical treatise, which he sent to the church at
Rome. I am especially thrilled with the verse in Romans
8:1, which says, "There is therefore now no condemnation to them which are in Christ Jesus, who walk not after
the flesh, but after the Spirit." I have frequently drama-
tized the verse by painting a verbal picture of a trial before
a circuit court judge in which Jesus is our defense attorney
and Father God is the judge. That is a winning combina-
tion, incapable of losing a case.

Describing this wonderful promise has sometimes
brought the congregation to their feet spontaneously as
they enthusiastically rejoiced in God, clapping their hands
and even shouting. It is awesome to actually realize that

Jesus has never lost a court case against us.

However, that was before my diagnosis of cancer. It was before the doctor pronounced me en route to a complete cure or, at least, to a satisfactory remission. And it was before the months of pain and the doctor's final verdict to "go home and die."

I had to learn to live through this new season in my life by following a spiritual principle taught to us in God's Word through the example of David—a man who faced incredibly difficult circumstances in his life but who learned the secret of maintaining his faith and trust in God by encouraging himself in the promises and provision of his God. "And David was greatly distressed...but David encouraged himself in the LORD his God" (1 Samuel 30:6).

It is human nature to sometimes forget to give thanks for blessings and dwell rather on our losses. Everyone does this at times. But the person who is plunged into a devastating life circumstance—such as a debilitating terminal illness, as in my case—will be tempted to dwell much longer upon the losses than is healthy, or God honoring to do. With David, I had to learn to encourage myself in the Lord. You will have to learn to live by that principle also. In this chapter I want to show you how I have learned to focus on the wonderful presence, promises, and provisions of my precious Lord and Savior. Because of Him, I can walk through this season with great joy and peace. You will be able to do the same.

LEAVING A LEGACY~*The Lord used your insights into worshiping years ago to waken my heart and eyes to His beauty and the joy of worshiping Him.*

THE POWER OF PRAISE

During the months that I have lived under a death sentence, I have continually "consumed" the Book of Psalms, searching for praise expressions and for new reasons to praise God. When I give priority to praise, there is neither time nor inclination for morbid self-examination. And I have found it impossible to condemn myself and praise God in the same breath.

Now when Satan, circumstances, or well-meaning friends try to heap guilt upon me, I fill my mind with reasons for praise and fill my mouth with expressions of praise. How thankful I am that I became a praiser long before I was diagnosed with cancer. With the perplexities and pain of my condition, at least I am not having to learn a new viewpoint for life; I have lived from the perspective of a praise-filled life for years. In my book *The Secret of Personal Prayer*, published in 1988, I told this story of a time when I learned the efficacy of praise in times of distress.

> A few years ago, I was fighting fatigue. I actually had to lift my legs with my hands to climb the stairs to my motel room. Deeply distressed, I threw myself across my bed and said, "God, this isn't right. I'm out of balance. You never intended me to wear out. Please help me." I slept well that night but, in the early hours of the morning, I had a dream: Someone I knew well sidled up to me in a church service and sang a new chorus to me. It was a paraphrase of 1 Corinthians 15:20. It exploded in my spirit. I awoke singing it. I sang it at breakfast, and, fearing that I would soon forget it, I wrote it on my napkin. All day long that chorus rang in my spirit with a rejoicing that was greater than I

had experienced in a long time. About church time, I realized that I was not tired. It proved to be the end of that season of extreme exhaustion. I had been healed with singing a "new song"…that brought my Lord and me into such intimate relationship that His presence could affect my physical body and restore me to strength.[1]

A praise-filled attitude was able to overcome my fatigue in 1988, and it has enabled me to walk through my process of dying. Praise works—when you are in the midst of a devastating life circumstance, turn your heart toward heaven and begin to praise God. Praise and worship will dominate our time in heaven. If that is so, shouldn't it be a beginning activity here on the earth? Most of the "religious" things we do on earth will not be done in eternity. There will be no buildings to construct, no special campaigns to conduct, no funds to be raised, no sermons to be preached. Every activity in heaven will center around the worship of God the Father, God the Son, and God the Holy Spirit.[2] When you face life's toughest moments, praise God! Make praise the focus of your life on earth just as it will be the focus of your life in heaven.

I have taught praise, written more than six books about praise, and have practiced praising God daily for many years. I can testify with David:

> He brought me up also out of an horrible pit, out of the miry clay, and set my feet upon a rock, and established my goings. And he hath put a new song in my mouth, even praise unto our God: many shall see it, and fear, and shall trust in the LORD.
>
> —PSALM 40:2–3

Remember that it is Jesus Christ whom we are praising. When we praise God on earth, we are merely practicing what we will be doing for an eternity in heaven. When we are released from Planet Earth and ushered into God's great heavens, what an inspiration to praise will meet us. When we stand with "ten thousand times ten thousand, and thousands of thousands" of angels (Revelation 5:11), and multitudes of people, "which no man could number, of all nations, and kindreds, and people, and tongues" (Revelation 7:9), how electrifying will be our praise motivation! When all the angels of God's creating stand around God's throne, and the four living creatures begin to lead the praise, while the twenty-four elders fall on their faces before the throne (Revelation 7:11), how could we help but be carried away in the vast spirit of worship and praise of that very hour![3]

And so we are able to insert a parenthesis in the midst of the eternity and interpolate our human, weak, fragile praise and know it will be incorporated forever into the worship of our heavenly Father. And since praise is eternal, it will likely take much of eternity to teach us all the truths about it.[4]

THE VALUE OF COMMEMORATING LIFE

I suppose that it is natural to play the "what if" game as we come to the end of life's journey. I fear that I am nearly a champion player. Since life is composed of many choices, we make it easy for us to wonder what the outcome might have been if our choices had been different. It has become glaringly obvious that every time I chose God's choices for my life, great good has come. He who knows the end from the beginning is in a great position to make good choices for our lives. Still, I am human enough to wonder "what if."

DYING WITH GRACE

As the day came to an end recently, Eleanor and I sat together in the family room and talked about what we may have missed in life. I felt that I might have missed some enjoyment of my boyhood days because of the "responsibility" of being a boy preacher. I also lamented that I didn't get a good quality college education. I have a keen intellect that could have handled the challenge of university studies. Though I have received two doctorate degrees, the one that is earned came from a small church college that isn't even in existence anymore. Another church college awarded me an honorary doctorate degree without my being present and even without my knowledge that it was being awarded.

I also complained that my circle of friends in the early years had been among the "lowly" Pentecostal people. I wondered if I might have achieved more in life if I had accepted the two invitations offered to me in my youth to enter the ministry according to the Methodist tradition.

One retiring Methodist minister told me he so regretted not having a son and that he would like to consider me as the son he didn't have. He offered to send me all the way through Methodist seminary. I refused his offer. A few years later, a second Methodist pastor made me a similar offer. When I refused it, he offered to place me in the largest Methodist church that could be pastored by a "lay pastor." His offer I also refused.

There is no way I can know what life would have been like if I had accepted either offer. I do have the assurance of knowing that, while I didn't get a university education or move up through the ranks of a large denomination, I did have the training of godly parents who knew God and walked in the ways of the Holy Spirit. Perhaps what I gleaned from their lives and what I learned from my father's teachings were sufficient for the ministry God had ordained for me.

And among the things I have never regretted is my introduction into what we now call the Charismatic movement. Because I was raised a Pentecostal, I stepped carefully into the Charismatic movement. But I quickly learned to love the liberty I found among the Charismatics. I am deeply indebted for my Pentecostal "wrappings," but I greatly love the life and vitality I have experienced among my fellow Charismatics.

We turned our conversation from what I may have missed in life to what I received from the time the doctor's death warrant was served until now. There were many blessings of this extended season of life for which to be thankful.

One of the blessings I have experienced is the joy of seeing God working profoundly in the lives of my children and grandchildren. I have a grandson-in-law I would not have had if my life had not been graciously extended. He married my wayward granddaughter and took on the responsibility of her three children, along with the son their marriage produced. When my granddaughter disappeared, leaving her children behind, we sent the two older children to live with their father, which has been a very healthy move. But my grandson-in-law offered to become a single father for the two preschool children. He is "Daddy" to them both, and they call me their "real Grandpa."

Had I gone home when *I* wanted to, what would have happened to these grandchildren? I am certain that God had another plan He could have executed, but instead, He kept me alive long enough to be an active participant in the rescue of these three lives.

Perhaps one of the greatest celebrations I have been able to commemorate in this season was when we went to Jeannie's (our middle daughter) home for a family meal with all three of our daughters and their husbands, five grandchildren, and five great-grandchildren. It may have been a little noisy, but it was a very joyous occasion. The meal was extra wonderful because Jeannie had recently remarried, and she is now happier than we have seen her in many years.

Jeannie, who had been single since her unhappy divorce some years earlier, had met a preacher whose wife had also left him. Jeannie and this interim minister found that they had many things in common. Both are very musical. Both have a passion for the work of the Lord. Both were lonely and discovered a genuine interest in each other.

Jeannie's son, David, has a lovely backyard that is tailor-made for a garden wedding. David erected a canopy in a corner of the yard that is "fenced in" with beautiful flowering shrubbery. The grandsons carried a large lounge chair into this canopy on which I could be seated—and the rest is history. I performed the wedding ceremony for my very happy daughter.

How kind the Lord has been to allow me to live long enough to see my daughter, who had been so severely wounded, get married again and be set on a pathway of restoration and health before taking me home. This happy event may pale in importance when I stand in the glorious presence of God in eternity. But right now in the measurement of space that we call "time," it is very important. It has been a very happy moment that my wife and I could share together in the here and now.

God has given me wonderful opportunities to be fruitful in the work of the Lord as well as in the precious lives of my family. Surprisingly, none of these earthly joys have dissipated the heavenly joys, which are becoming more and more real to me each day.

ALLOWING GOD'S WORD
TO PERMEATE MY SOUL

When I entered this season, I discovered that instead of the imminent death for which I waited, I was regaining my strength. In life, I have always been a Bible reader. I usually read the Scriptures in their entirety each year along with reading the Book of Psalms every month. As I began to regain strength, my son-in-law Norbert purchased a large print Bible for me. What a joy it was to return to reading the blessed Book.

Having nothing else to do during this time I was still awaiting death, I managed to read the Bible through three times during the first year after the doctor's ultimatum, and I continued to read the Book of Psalms each month. Reading the Word of God was an amazing source of strength for me—spiritually, emotionally, and even physically. I found the psalmist to be accurate when he wrote: "The *entrance of thy words* giveth light; it giveth understanding unto the simple" (Psalm 119:130, emphasis added).

I was seeking understanding; I even searched the ancient Book of Job. This great patriarch of the faith and I shared a few similarities, but our dissimilarities are far greater than those similarities. I received more help from the messages of the Psalms, perhaps because even without the answers I craved, I could consistently relate to David's perplexed cries and then join him in his praises to God.

Throughout this book I have sprinkled Scripture verses that minister greatly to my spirit. You will be able to use these living words to lift your spirit also, and I encourage you to discover the strength of God's Word for yourself.

As I have already stated, the Book of Psalms has always been one of my favorite places to go in God's Word to find encouragement. Through this season of my life, I have found a number of verses from Psalms to be especially hope producing and spirit lifting. When you are feeling discouraged and need encouragement from God, use this section of favorite psalms to help you once again find your source of strength and peace in God.

Spirit Lifters From the Book of Psalms

Hear me when I call, O God of my righteousness: thou hast enlarged me when I was in distress; have mercy upon me, and hear my prayer.

—Psalm 4:1

But know that the Lord hath set apart him that is godly for himself: the Lord will hear when I call unto him.

—Psalm 4:3

Thou wilt shew me the path of life: in thy presence is fulness of joy; at thy right hand there are pleasures for evermore.

—Psalm 16:11

Thou has proved mine heart; thou hast visited me in the night; thou has tried me, and shalt find nothing; I am purposed that my mouth shall not transgress.

—Psalm 17:3

I will call upon the Lord, who is worthy to be praised: so shall I be saved from mine enemies.

—Psalm 18:3

With the merciful thou wilt shew thyself merciful; with an upright man thou wilt shew thyself upright.

—PSALM 18:25

As for God, his way is perfect: the word of the LORD is tried: he is a buckler to all those that trust in him.

—PSALM 18:30

For in the time of trouble he shall hide me in his pavilion: in the secret of his tabernacle shall he hide me; he shall set me up upon a rock.

—PSALM 27:5

But the salvation of the righteous is of the LORD: he is their strength in the time of trouble. And the LORD shall help them, and deliver them: he shall deliver them from the wicked, and save them, because they trust in him.

—PSALM 37:39–40

PREPARING MYSELF FOR MINISTRY IN THIS SEASON

At the temple gate called Beautiful, Peter told the lame man sitting there and begging alms, "Such as I have give I thee" (Acts 3:6). Peter's declaration is an equation the Holy Spirit reminds me of regularly. I can't give something unless I have it. Also, if I have given it away to another, I don't have it anymore. How useless it is to try to give to one person what you have already given to another.

This means that I must prepare myself every day for ministry to myself, to God, and to others. No matter how prepared I may have been when I retired for the night, I have to prepare myself afresh in the morning for the assignments of the day.

No two days are identical for me. Today I awoke with such pain in my side that I forced myself to get out of bed before I could completely open my eyes. My legs ached, and I feared they wouldn't hold me upright.

I reached for my cane to help steady me as I walked the short distance to the bathroom. Neither leg wanted to move, and I heard myself ask out loud, "Is it worth it?" Every morning I fight pain levels that are extremely severe before I take my first medication. Breakfast is required before the pills can be swallowed. Then patience must prevail as those pills take their own sweet time to deliver the much needed relief.

On this day, it would have been so easy to fall back into bed. No one would have condemned me for doing so. But I can't write this book in bed. Furthermore, I don't know who may come by today or what other divinely ordained assignments await me.

Painfully, I almost dragged myself to my toothbrush, comb, and razor. I then walked to the electric cart my brother loaned to me and drove myself to the family room.

After a bowl of oatmeal and a cup of coffee, my bathing nurse helped me into the shower for a good scrubbing and then helped me get dressed. I don't think anyone would condemn me for remaining in my nightgown all day, but I choose to wear a shirt, tie, a pair of slacks, and my dress shoes each day. It helps my frame of mind to be dressed up all day. I feel physically ready for whatever might come my way.

Now it is time to minister to God. Actually, this ministry begins the moment my feet touch the floor when I ask, "Jesus, please help me." While brushing my teeth, I am mentally praising the Lord for strength to care for my physical needs, and my electric shaver seems to echo my praise to God.

While eating breakfast, I usually find a preacher on television and rejoice with him as he expounds God's Word. When I'm back to my lounge chair following my bath and getting dressed, it is time to read five psalms for the day. How life producing these psalms have become to me. Often a verse reaches out and grabs me—it becomes my theme for the day.

Having ministered to myself and to God, I am now ready to minister to others. It is time to turn on my laptop computer, reach for my portable dictating recorder to answer today's e-mails, or answer the phone.

Speaking of the phone, I secured an 800 number to make calling home easier when I was traveling. Now that I am confined to my house, it would save a few dollars each month if I would cancel this service, but I have found a wonderful use for this telephone expense as a ministry tool. There are widows of minister friends of mine who are getting by on a very limited budget, and they are lonely. I have given them this toll-free number so they can call me at any time. It seems to be a great source of joy for them, and it isn't a heavy financial burden for me. None has abused this privilege so far. It is also a blessing to my wife's sister who lives in California.

My bathing nurse just came by to tell me that the bed has been made and she is leaving. She stood in front of me with her right hand extended, waiting for me to pray for her. It's a simple ministry, but it is a ministry. Who else is going to bring a touch of God into her life today?

When I was the pastor of a church, and later a traveling minister, I used to prepare myself adequately before trying to preach in the pulpit. I studied faithfully, I prayed fervently, and I spoke earnestly. I did not attempt to "minister off the cuff."

Now that ministry is usually one-to-one, I feel I still

must prepare myself to the best of my ability. I never know how important any contact may be. And I appreciate more deeply the many times Jesus ministered to a single person as recorded in the Scriptures.

Before my prayers are ended by the call for me to "come up higher," I want my "earth," my physical body in which God's Spirit has taken residence, to be completely filled with God's glory. So much so that everyone with whom I come into contact can be aware of God's loving, redeeming presence. In the final psalm accredited to David, we read:

> Blessed be the LORD God, the God of Israel, who only doeth wondrous things. And blessed be his glorious name for ever: and let the whole earth be filled with his glory; Amen, and Amen. The prayers of David the son of Jesse are ended.
> —PSALM 72:18–20

It is likely that David meant the physical earth should be filled with God's glory, but could it not also refer to our earthly bodies? I want that glory to outshine the pain I am suffering or the physical limitations that restrict me in so many ways.

When Jesus was on the earth, God's glory radiated out of Him regardless of the circumstances in which we view Him. May God grant me a similar divine grace. I believe that dying grace begins with grace for living. I seriously question whether I will experience a dying grace if I have not learned to appropriate God's grace to live in my present circumstances, no matter how unpleasant they may be. And if I cannot live successfully in that grace, it is obvious that I cannot minister that grace to others.

As we all get older, I believe the Twenty-third Psalm becomes more personal to us. We can take comfort in knowing that the final pasture in which we will feed has been chosen by our Shepherd. He knows that we don't have enough wisdom to rest properly, so, "he maketh me to lie down in green pastures" (Psalm 23:2). We ran and frolicked in the green grass as a lamb, and I think our Shepherd enjoyed watching us, but as mature sheep, we have work to do. We are expected to grow wool—to produce "life" for the benefit of others.

I believe that I have been a faithful wool producer during the years of my ministry. I remember wondering what would happen to me when I got too old to grow any more wool. How would I survive when I became too infirm to gather enough food for myself?

Years ago, one day the Lord spoke to me when I was musing on this very real concern about my future. "Judson," the Lord said to me by His Spirit, "I don't love you for what you can *do* for Me. I love you—period. No matter how much you do in My kingdom, you will always be an 'unprofitable servant' (Luke 17:10). Because of My love for you, when you become so infirm that you cannot feed yourself, I will pull grass in the pasture and hand feed you." I can now attest to the fulfillment of that promise.

LEAVING A LEGACY~ *Thank you for sharing and expounding God's Word with the body of Christ. I appreciate the stand you take on worship.*

EXPERIENCING THE LORD'S TABLE

Part of the process of learning to encourage ourselves in the Lord has been the joy of experiencing His provision for our daily needs. Eleanor and I were very young as we suffered through the Great Depression years in America. We learned to live frugally early in life. My wife can still squeeze a penny so tightly that it makes President Lincoln squirm. Those early lessons of financial responsibility have continued to be a priority throughout our lives. For example, for several years, we made double or larger mortgage payments on our house. That made it possible, when we moved to Phoenix, to purchase a twenty-year-old tract house without needing to finance it with a mortgage. We prefer to have older merchandise we can afford rather than new things for which we have to go into debt.

When honorariums were being paid freely, we also chose to invest some of that money in a savings account. We knew that I could not continue to travel forever. We didn't expect, however, that my traveling schedule would collapse so soon because of my health.

Then, as we faced the likelihood of my death, we were thankful to have everything paid for and to have a few thousand dollars in the bank. However, with the loss of my breadwinner status in the family, we knew these limited resources wouldn't last forever. As I gained more strength, I discussed these financial issues with Eleanor. I felt we needed to draw up a budget that would make the available funds last the maximum length of time possible.

On the plus side, not only were we debt free, but also we still had some outside sources of income. There was the interest on the CDs; my books were still selling and paying me royalties; some videotaped courses I had taught for CLST (Christian Life School of Theology in Columbus, Georgia) were paying me quarterly honorariums; and we have a few partners who faithfully send monthly checks as an investment in my ministry.

If we greatly tightened our belts, we calculated that we could get by for a few years. One consideration was to do without my secretary, but that would mean closing my office. This scenario did not, however, make room for medical expenses for either of us. In my weakened condition, this financial situation loomed before me as a big problem.

Then the Twenty-third Psalm came alive to my spirit afresh, in which David addresses the Lord (my Shepherd) in the second person: "Thou preparest a table before me..." (Psalm 23:5). David characterized the Good Shepherd as the One who takes the responsibility for having an ample food supply for His sheep. As I mused on this, I remembered God's promise to me. "Judson," He said firmly and kindly, "I feed old sheep, too."

God reinforced this comforting promise of His provision with the words that conclude the report of Psalm 78: "So *he fed them* according to the integrity of his heart; and guided them by the skilfulness of his hands" (verse 72, emphasis added).

Some years ago, I read a report that said it would have daily taken over forty freight trains loaded to full capacity to feed Israel in the wilderness. And they needed twice that amount on Friday, for they had to gather enough manna on Friday to feed them on both Friday and the Sabbath day.

My daily needs are a tiny fraction of what their needs were. Still, just as the Israelites had to exhibit faith by going to the manna fields each morning, so I have to exercise faith on a daily basis for my financial provision.

No doubt you have faced some of these same financial challenges during this season of illness yourself. Perhaps you have been tempted to worry and fear that your material sustenance will not be able to provide for the financial need that you and your loved ones will face—or are facing. It is important that you recognize that God is your Provider—your Jehovah Jireh. Encourage yourself in His promise to provide for all your needs, and trust Him to answer you in your day of need in unexpected ways. He will not let you down.

For the first few months after the word of my death sentence was released, we received phone calls and letters from individuals and churches pledging financial help on a monthly basis. I must confess that I responded fearfully—expecting this to run out very quickly. But it hasn't. These generous pledges have been paid faithfully month by month.

Getting the mail now has a new excitement in it. We wonder how much support the Lord has provided today. Almost every mail delivery becomes a new reason for praise and thanksgiving.

And there have been special miracles along the way. A few months ago, we faced an unusually large expenditure. To my amazement—"Lord, please forgive my little faith"—I received a letter from one of my publishers telling me that the rights to one of my books had been sold to a European publisher. My remuneration for this transaction was an enclosed check for several thousand dollars. God was right on time!

My worry that the cost of the medications they were giving to me would "eat me out of house and home" was negated when I discovered that all the hospice expenses, including nurses and medications, were paid for through Social Security. That is better than money in the bank for me, because I do not have to pay taxes on it.

Is God faithful? You had better believe it. There are two aging sheep here in Phoenix who are living daily in God's ample provision. He has proven to us personally that He feeds old sheep, too. We are enjoying our daily experience of feasting at His table.

1. Cornwall, *The Secret of Personal Prayer*, 173–174.
2. Ibid., 196.
3. Judson Cornwall, *Let Us Praise* (North Brunswick, NJ: Bridge-Logos Publishers, 1973), 136.
4. Ibid.

KEY PRINCIPLE

Eternal life with God is a reward so
wonderful, in our finiteness, we cannot
grasp its beauty.

For I am in a strait betwixt two, having a desire to depart, and to be with Christ; which is far better.

—PHILIPPIANS 1:23

Chapter 8

Embarking for Heaven

I go to prepare a place for you. And if I go and prepare a place for you, I will come again, and receive you unto myself; that where I am, there ye may be also.

—John 14:2–3

The moment of stepping from this life into the next should not be one we dread or fear. That is the moment for which every child of God is waiting. It will be a very quick process, a joyful process. Instantly we are caught up into the presence of God. Jesus said that He would be there to gather us; He will meet us. This life on earth is nothing more than a short-term time of preparation for our eternal life in heaven. Heaven is God's home, His abode, and He is going to share that home with me— with you. His presence with me will be the joy of heaven.

I want to help you to know what I have learned about preparing to embark on my trip to heaven. No, I don't want to tell you what possessions to purchase for the trip, what luggage to pack, or what airline to travel on. During my life on this earth, I have spent countless hours traveling on every airline flying in the skies above this earth. But not one of those planes had the capacity to transport me to my heavenly home.

The preparation we must make to make that final trip to heaven does not involve any of the trappings of this life on earth. Our preparation for heaven is much more important than any preparations you may have completed for a trip in this earthly realm in which we live. We must be prepared to enter a different realm—a spiritual realm where we will live forever with our Lord.

I am afraid that today's generation of Christians is so totally caught up with the here and now that we are no longer concerned with the hereafter. We have become very materialistically oriented. As I was growing up through the Great Depression years, we didn't have much of anything in this realm, so it was rather natural to be looking for something better in the realm to come. But in many ways, today we have abandoned that joyful hope in the hereafter for an embracing of the things we seek in the here and now. The reality of this life is that it is nothing more than a preparatory period for the hereafter. God has given us a life here to prepare our hearts for the life there.

LEAVING A LEGACY~*I hope you know how often you inspire me and how much I look up to you for the difference you make just by being who you are.*

During my lifetime of service to my Lord, I have been doing my best to prepare for heaven. But that preparation rose to an entirely new level when I received my death sentence from the lips of my doctor. Many months have passed since that moment. How long has it been since your death sentence was served? Have you, like me, realized that you had precious few moments left to make your final preparations for the moment when you will step from this life into eternity? Are you prepared to embark for heaven?

A Mandatory Death Sentence Awaits All Men

"I haven't been served a death warrant yet," you may say. You are wrong. Perhaps physically you are not facing death, as I am. However, the Bible teaches us that when Adam, the first representative of mankind, sinned in the Garden of Eden, his sin brought death to the entire human race. Not only did natural death to our physical bodies enter the scene, but spiritual death, involving eternal separation from God, also became a sad reality for all of mankind. My death sentence issued by the doctor is not as devastating as the death sentence over every life that has not acknowledged this biblical reality of eternal damnation, referred to in Scripture as the "second death" (Revelation 20:12–14).

Theologians refer to mankind's universal "death sentence" as the "Adamic sin" or "original" sin. Many people reject this spiritual reality, saying that Adam's sin couldn't possibly affect them. Unfortunately for them, their declaration doesn't change the teaching of the Bible that declares, "…in Adam all die" (1 Corinthians 15:22). This reference is not merely to the fact of physical death, but also to the reality of eternal separation from God.

When we are tempted to refute the truth of biblical teaching, we need to remember the words of the apostle Paul: "Yea, let God be true, but every man a liar" (Romans 3:4). The Scriptures clearly teach that every person born lives under the curse of Adamic sin. So it follows that we have also received his death sentence, of which God clearly warned Adam, saying:

> Of every tree of the garden thou mayest freely
> eat: But of the tree of the knowledge of good

115

and evil, thou shalt not eat of it: for in the day
that thou eatest thereof thou shalt surely die.

—GENESIS 2:16–17

It seems so simple an obedience, especially assuming the
state of innocence in which Adam and Eve lived, without
the terrible "propensity" for sin we suffer. Yet, the powerful
enemy of our souls, Satan himself, speaking through the
serpent, was able to deceive Eve, and this first couple chose
to disbelieve God's Word and disobey His command. And
what God promised, He had to do. From that day to this,
the curse of death has been imputed to every person.

For the sake of argument, however, suppose that we are
not under the Adamic curse. Nothing much would change.
According to the Scriptures, we are all still under a personal death sentence. Twice the Old Testament prophet
Ezekiel wrote, "The soul that sinneth, it shall die" (Ezekiel
18:4, 20). That verdict is fairly clear. I don't think any person living would declare they have never sinned in
thought, word, or deed.

And in the New Testament, the writer of the Book of
Hebrews warns us, "It is appointed unto men once to die,
but after this the judgment" (Hebrews 9:27). This statement is equally indisputable. Each of us has been served a
death warrant, which we cannot escape. No one is going
to get out of this world alive, with the exception of those
who have been born again and are living when Christ
returns in the Rapture. Those happy souls will be caught
up to meet Him in the air (1 Thessalonians 4:17).

For the rest, we are going to die physically—every one of
us—and following death is the judgment for both the righteous and the unrighteous. That judgment will determine
your fate for eternity, whether eternal life with God or eternal damnation separated from God. You will not be able to

talk your way out of this eternal death sentence, for God is the Judge and the Holy Spirit is the Prosecuting Attorney. They know your innermost thoughts and every action of your life. Again, it is the writer to the Hebrews who makes this reality painfully clear:

> For the word of God is quick, and powerful, and sharper than any twoedged sword, piercing even to the dividing asunder of soul and spirit, and of the joints and marrow, and is a *discerner of the thoughts and intents of the heart.* Neither is there any creature that is not manifest in his sight: but *all things are naked and opened unto the eyes of him with whom we have to do.*
> —HEBREWS 4:12–13, EMPHASIS ADDED

As you stand before God, you will realize that you actually have no defense. You will not be able to successfully plead ignorance, for your conscience will testify against you. It is useless to plead good works, for there is nothing any one of us can do to atone for sin. (See Ephesians 2:7–9.) According to the Bible, only Christ's blood atones for sin and iniquity. Unless you have accepted His sacrifice for sin by making Him Lord and Savior of your life, you will stand before that judgment seat of Christ and be judged "guilty" before you even open your mouth.

"But that is unfair," you may protest. Is it? Look at the great grace and mercy that God has extended to me these days since my physical death warrant was served. This same God of love is offering unlimited grace and mercy to you every day that you live. His only Son took the punishment for your sins that *you* deserve. It remains only for you to accept Christ as Savior, ask Him to forgive your sins, and determine to serve Him. Not only will you be saved from the judgment of eternal damnation, but you will also begin to discover the destiny for your life ordained by God Himself.

The Lord is not a harsh, retributive God who delights in extracting every possible ounce of punishment from us. He has revealed Himself as a tender, loving, compassionate God who loves us so much that He, in Christ Jesus, actually became human so that as the God/man, He could die in our place to release us from the penalty, power, and presence of sin in our lives.

However, we dare not wait for Him to show us mercy when we stand before Him at the judgment seat. He extends that mercy to us in life now, not in the hereafter. To avoid eternal separation from God, we must accept God's provision for eternal life during our lifetime.

REVERSING THE DEATH SENTENCE

How wonderful it is that the Bible, which serves our death warrant, also offers us a reprieve from that warrant. The same verse that declares, "For the wages of sin is death," adds, "but the *gift of God* is eternal life through Jesus Christ our Lord" (Romans 6:23, emphasis added).

LEAVING A LEGACY~You have stamped and molded our congregation. You are always a spiritual father to me and this church.

We inherited the sentence of death from Adam, and we earned more through our personal sin. But in spite of that, what we are offered is life—eternal life.

God magnanimously cancels His own law when we accept His love gift of salvation through Christ's shed blood. The apostle Paul explains, "But God commendeth His love toward us, in that, while we were yet sinners, Christ died for us" (Romans 5:8). He goes on to say that we are saved from the wrath of God through the sacrifice of Christ.

The apostle Peter told us, "The Lord is not slack concerning his promise, as some men count slackness; but is longsuffering to us-ward, not willing that *any should perish*, but that all should come to repentance" (2 Peter 3:9, emphasis added).

Peter makes two major emphases in this verse. First, he reminds us that God is uncompromising in what He promises. That is good news when, through repentance, we place our lives under the Lordship of Christ in order to receive mercy and inherit the promise of eternal life. In the negative, however, never think you can talk God out of His promised judgment. Though He is longsuffering, delaying His judgment as long as possible, the fact is, if He said it, He will do it.

Second, the apostle tells us that God is unwilling that anyone perish. The only way these two truths—God's mercy and His judgment—can be reconciled is for you to choose repentance as the only way to avert God's death sentence. Asking Christ to forgive your sin allows His precious blood to cleanse you and reconcile you to God's love (Romans 5:10).

And it is important to understand that, while repentance may begin with a godly sorrow for sin, true repentance involves much more than an emotional response in recognition of personal sin. It will affect our lifestyle. By definition, repentance involves an "about face" in our march through life. Repentance causes us to forsake our own way to embrace God's way; our "lordship" for His. Repentance results in a radical realignment of belief and behavior. It enables us to become new creatures in Christ Jesus.

Is it worth it to surrender my sinful ways and submit my life to the Lordship of Christ? Emphatically yes! When we turn from sin, whether we view that sin as minor or major, we will receive a renewed hope of living eternally with Jesus and with friends and loved ones who have preceded us into heaven. Our death warrant, which has been served, no longer holds any power over our eternal destiny to live forever in the presence of God.

Anticipating Heaven

In my book *Heaven*, I state, "Heaven is a real place, prepared for real people, who will enjoy its benefits in real bodies."[1]

It is not without significance that an inner awareness of a real heaven has been placed so strongly in the heart of man that there is not a single religion on the face of the earth that does not make a provision for a heaven. The view and concept of that heaven varies greatly, but some sort of utopia beyond this life must be offered to satisfy the inner craving that exists. God, the Creator, programmed into man strong desires for what would be available to him and good for him. Among these many drives, or instincts, that God has built into the human being is a belief in and a yearning for heaven. These very yearnings argue favorably for the existence of a literal, real heaven that will satisfy these God-given cravings, for, in satisfying every other propensity with which we were born, we have found substance and reality. Surely there is an actuality to meet this craving as well. God would never cause us to desire a heaven if there were no heaven to satisfy that desire.[2]

The apostle Paul, who was granted a glimpse into heaven, said this:

> For we know that when this tent we live in now is taken down—when we die and leave these bodies—we will have wonderful new bodies in heaven, homes that will be ours forevermore, made for us by God himself, and not by human hands. How weary we grow of our present

bodies. That is why we look forward eagerly to
the day when we shall have heavenly bodies
which we shall put on like new clothes. For we
shall not be merely spirits without bodies.
These earthly bodies make us groan and sigh,
but we wouldn't like to think of dying and having no bodies at all. We want to slip into our
new bodies so that these dying bodies will, as it
were, be swallowed up by everlasting life. This
is what God has prepared for us and, as a guar-
antee, he has given us his Holy Spirit.
—2 CORINTHIANS 5:1–5, TLB

Those who have died in Christ have not been cheated out
of life; they have been metamorphosed into the real life. And
the best part about that real life will be seeing Jesus face to
face. John tells us, "We shall see him as he is" (1 John 3:2).

Heaven would be glorious even without this, but after
seeing Him as He really is—not as we have imagined Him
to be—heaven's joys will be absolutely overwhelming.
Moses is the only man in the Bible who was afforded the
privilege of face-to-face communication with God, but in
heaven it will be available to all of us. If just knowing Him
through the letters He wrote (the Bible) has made Christ so
precious, try to picture what it will do to us when we actually behold Him intimately.

In *Heaven*, I tried to describe what this will be like for us:

We shall see Him "face to face." This is the basis
for our hope and the blessing of that hope—
interpersonal relationship with Christ Jesus our
Lord. This will complete the circle of time,
placing it into the circuit of eternity. The era of
God and man walking and talking together in
Paradise's garden which was lost through
Adam's fall will be restored again, and God's

original purpose of creation will be realized—
fellowship between creature and creator with
complete understanding, compassionate caring,
and companionate sharing. Now we only sing
about it: "Face to face shall I behold him"—
"And he walks with me, and he talks with me"—
"And I shall see him face to face"—but in heaven
we'll experience it, and much more![3]

The best is yet to come! "Eye hath not seen, nor ear
heard, neither have entered into the heart of man, the
things which God hath prepared for them that love him.
But God hath revealed them unto us by his Spirit"
(1 Corinthians 2:9–10), and this limited revelation is
enough to excite the overcoming Christian to renewed
faith and hope, for better days are ahead for all of us.[4]

EXPECT EXODUS BY DESIGN

One of the most comforting verses in the entire Word of
God is John 14:2–3, which says, "I go to prepare a place
for you. And if I go and prepare a place for you, I will
come again, and receive you unto myself; that where I am,
there ye may be also."

It is difficult to use the word *exodus* without immediately
thinking about the children of Israel coming out of Egypt
to journey to the Promised Land. It is awesome to me that
every step of this great transfer of over four million people
across the wilderness was planned and directed by God.

Each of us faces an exodus of our own, a day when we
will exit life as we know it and enter another realm of life.
The timing of our transfer from one form of life to another
is unknown, but its reality is as certain as this morning's
sunrise. And when it happens, we will leave our "slavery in
Egypt" and head toward God's promised land—heaven.

God has planned our exodus down to the most minute detail. As we discussed, our transfer from earth to heaven may occur in one of two ways—through death or in the Rapture. Only those believers who are alive when Christ returns will go up in the Rapture. All others will enter heaven through the portals of death.

A DIVINE APPOINTMENT

I can almost feel you shudder as you read that word—*death*. We all seem to have an innate fear of death. We do everything in our power to escape it, but there is no escape from it. We prefer to live in denial of its reality; but that pretense is futile. We referred earlier to the Bible's declaration that "it is appointed unto men once to die" (Hebrews 9:27). God made this appointment, and He will see to it that you keep it.

It is, of course, popular to declare victory over death, whether by medicine or by faith. Just this morning I heard a popular television preacher declare that we do not need to die. He propounded that if our faith is strong enough we can live forever. This message has been preached since I was a little boy, but the preachers who declared it eventually died, in spite of their solemn faith. So will this man. Death is a divine appointment that cannot be broken. We all will die!

What then? What will death be like? What awaits us on the other side of death?

GOD'S PERSPECTIVE OF DEATH

We need to see how God views death. It seems that God's original intent for humanity was for believers to undergo metamorphosis into the very image of God, much as the caterpillar that emerges from his cocoon as a beautiful butterfly.

Originally God created mankind so that He could have a family that bore His likeness. "And God said, Let us make man in our image, after our likeness" (Genesis 1:26). It is likely that Enoch exemplified God's plan, for after living a long and productive life he was translated into the very presence of God. We read, "And Enoch walked with God: and he was not; for God took him" (Genesis 5:24). Enoch stepped from the natural world into the spiritual realm—from one form of being to another.

Paul wrote, "A man...is the image and glory of God" (1 Corinthians 11:7), and he assures us that "as we have borne the image of the earthy, we shall also bear the image of the heavenly" (1 Corinthians 15:49). Hallelujah! We, like Enoch, shall yet bear God's image. Sin did not destroy God's desire to have children like Himself; it only postponed its fulfillment.

God's wonderful plan for our redemption gave our personal larvae new life. Paul wrote, "For as in Adam all die, even so in Christ shall all be made alive" (1 Corinthians 15:22). So, the first step in God's plan is for our spirits to be made alive through the new birth. As Jesus explained to the teacher of the Jews, Nicodemus, "Except a man be born of water and of the Spirit, he cannot enter into the kingdom of God. That which is born of the flesh is flesh; and that which is born of the Spirit is spirit. Marvel not that I said unto thee, Ye must be born again" (John 3:5–7).

Once the sin issue has been settled, we become new creatures in Christ Jesus—we live as new creatures. (See 2 Corinthians 5:17.) This eternal transaction is very tangible. The apostle Paul assures us:

> The Spirit itself beareth witness with our spirit, that we are the children of God: and if children, then heirs; heirs of God, and joint-heirs

with Christ; if so be that we suffer with him,
that we may be also glorified together.

—ROMANS 8:16–17

We are children of God awaiting our transfer to the
Father's house. We have the mind and nature of Christ that
yearns to be with Jesus. This divine perspective of life
changes our perspective of death.

Dr. Jeremiah, in a television sermon, declared: "We are
not the living going on to the dying; we are the dying
going on to the living." How wondrously true this is.
According to God's plan for our exodus, we will be trans-
formed from the lower to the higher; from the mortal into
the immortal; and from the terrestrial (earthly) into the
celestial (heavenly).

My friend LaMar Boschman wrote to me a few days after
I received my death sentence. He said, "Remember, we are
not human beings having a temporary spiritual experience,
but we are spiritual beings having a temporary human experience. You will transcend the mundane and carnal and
behold the majestic and mysterious."

This supernatural change will occur before we even get
into heaven. God's Word declares:

> In a moment, in the twinkling of an eye, at the
> last trump: for the trumpet shall sound, and
> the dead shall be raised incorruptible, and we
> shall be changed. For this corruptible must
> put on incorruption, and this mortal must put
> on immortality. So when this corruptible shall
> have put on incorruption, and this mortal
> shall have put on immortality, then shall be
> brought to pass the saying that is written,
> Death is swallowed up in victory.
>
> —1 CORINTHIANS 15:52–54

Consider the good news of that last statement: "Death is swallowed up in victory." God views death as a victory, not a defeat. It is a personal trumpet call to come out of Egypt—our present habitation—and head for the promised land—heaven. But what is our destination like? I will admit that I do not know.

The beauties of heaven and unhindered life with God Himself defy our imagination. I have read the testimonies of several who have had near-death experiences that took them into heaven, and each was significantly different from the others. How wisely does the Bible declare, "Eye hath not seen, nor ear heard, neither have entered into the heart of man, the things which God hath prepared for them that love him" (1 Corinthians 2:9).

The Scriptures do give us a few glimpses beyond the veil. John, the beloved disciple, gives us quite a graphic picture of heaven in the Book of Revelation. He presents it as a beautiful city with walls of jasper and streets of gold. Much earlier in my ministry, I wrote an entire book on John's picture of heaven. It is titled simply: *Heaven*.

What I do not know about heaven far exceeds what I do know about it, however, and this only intensifies my desire to go there. All who have been given even brief glimpses into this beautiful abode prepared by God for His saints do their best to describe the indescribable and to explain the inexplicable. They are about as handicapped as a person living in the days of Christ would be if he were suddenly catapulted into our time frame of living and, upon his return, would try to describe our way of life to his contemporaries. They would view things so natural to our lifestyle as supernatural, and some things would be beyond their powers of description. So is heaven to us.

To understand spiritual mysteries requires a point of reference for them to even be describable. We have no such point of reference available to us, for heaven is so unlike earth as to defy even our wildest imaginations.

But we can still try! Close your eyes, and mentally visualize the most beautiful scene you can. Fill it with flowers, animals, people, or whatever is heavenly to you. Surround yourself with angels, and mentally visualize the presence of God. Perhaps you can hear music so beautiful as to evoke tears of joy, while seeing colors so vivid that they seem to almost speak to you. Sniff the aroma that only heaven could produce, and then multiply this ecstasy by a million times, and you would still be far from an accurate description of the heaven God has prepared for His children.

Want to go? I do! The final pages of our Bible tells us that in heaven there will be no pain, no sickness, no sorrow, nothing that defiles, and no darkness, for the Lamb of God is the light of this great city.

Again, what I don't know far exceeds what I do know. I don't know where this New Jerusalem, this heaven, is located or how to get there. I don't need to know, for at the moment of my death, as my spirit leaves my cancer-ridden body to enter the glorified body God has prepared for it, Jesus will be there to escort me to the home He has prepared for me. He told His disciples and us:

> I go to prepare a place for you. And if I go and prepare a place for you, I will come again, and receive you unto myself; that where I am, there ye may be also.
> —JOHN 14:2–3

Maybe my faith is too simple, but I find these words to be very satisfactory to me. For Jesus to meet me at the moment of my death and take me to be with Him forever will be heaven to me. And remember, He does what He promises. His promise is an exodus by design.

What great grace it will be to live forever with Jesus. But that is a grace He has given to me in my here and now also. Yet, incredible as it seems, I enjoy His loving presence before I die. I am especially conscious of the nearness of His presence now that I have been made aware of how near my exodus is.

God has given me great grace to live with cancer, which has greatly restricted my natural life and my ministry lifestyle. Very shortly, He will give me sufficient grace to step from this life into the next one. Do I now have that grace? I doubt it, but I don't need it now.

I am discovering that His grace is both sufficient and available when it is needed. I will lack nothing I need to make the death transition into endless life with God. The timing and the method are all in God's hands, and He does all things well. I am packed and ready, and when He comes by, I will go with Him into His eternal provision for my life. Why don't you get packed and go with me?

1. Judson Cornwall, *Heaven* (Essex, England: Sharon Publications, LTD., 1989), 18.
2. Ibid., 18–19.
3. Ibid., 128.
4. Ibid., 135.
5. Ibid.

Power-up your days with prayer

We pray that you found inner strength and peace in reading this important message by Dr. Cornwall. He has written many incredible books, but here is one that specifically needs to be in your library.

Words Cannot Express...

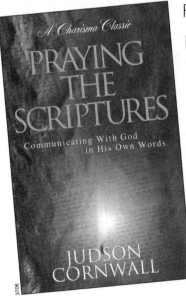

Frustrated by your limited prayer vocabulary? Expand your expressions of adoration and devotion using verses from the Psalms, the letters of Paul, and Jesus' own prayers to the Father.

Open your Bible, and raise your petitions with new-found joy, power, and under-standing.

$11.99 / 0-88419-266-0

Strang Communications, the publisher of both Charisma House and *Charisma* magazine, wants to give you a FREE SUBSCRIPTION to our award-winning magazine.

Since its inception in 1975, *Charisma* magazine has helped thousands of Christians stay connected with what God is doing worldwide.

Within its pages you will discover in-depth reports and the latest news from a Christian perspective, biblical health tips, global events in the body of Christ, personality profiles, and so much more. Join the family of *Charisma* readers who enjoy feeding their spirit each month with miracle-filled testimonies and inspiring articles that bring clarity, provoke prayer, and demand answers.

To claim your **3 free issues** of *Charisma,* send us your name and address to: Charisma 3 Free Issue Offer, 600 Rinehart Road, Lake Mary, FL 32746. Or you may call 1-800-829-3346 and ask for Offer # 93FREE. This offer is only valid in the USA.

www.charismamag.com